THIS IS A CARLTON BOOK

© Rubik © Seven Towns Ltd

Rubik and Rubik's are trademarks of Seven Towns Ltd., used under license.

Text and design copyright © Carlton Books Limited 1999

This edition published by Carlton Books Limited 1999

A CIP Catalogue for this book is available from the British Library

ISBN 1 85868 790 X

Executive Editor: Tim Dedopulos
Design: Paul Messam
Art Editor: Adam Wright
Production: Alexia Turner

Printed and bound in Italy

RUBIK'S PUZZLES

ALBIE FIORE WITH LÁSZLÓ MÉRÖ

CARLTON

Contents

INTRODUCTION TO RUBIK'S PUZZLES

Dear Reader,

It is almost exactly a quarter century that I created my Cube, little realising at the time the impact it would have on the world of puzzles and beyond.

Much has happened in the intervening years. Inspired by the same idea, a whole generation of 3D brain teasers – some originated by me and some by others – have captured the imagination of the public. The increasing popularity of Video and CD ROM games has reached the field of puzzles, and now you can play with and learn to master my Cube on the little screen.

Yet, throughout these technological and cultural changes, my little six-coloured Cube not only survived but became one of those classic toys that you would expect to find in any decent retail outlet. At the same time, the traditional 'paper and pencil' puzzle has also withstood the effects of the fast evolving environment, and has proved its enduring popularity.

In the course of the last twenty years I have met some of the most distinguished puzzle solvers and puzzle setters and worked with the finest brains across the entire gamut of the puzzle domain. In the course of these many varied collaborations I have often wondered about the relationship between 2D and 3D puzzles. I was intrigued by the question of the similarity in thought processes that sets and attempts to resolve problems in the two media.

I have always believed that the best to way to try answer a theoretical question is by practical experiment. So I have asked two of my friends, both deeply steeped in the culture of 'paper and pencil' puzzles to compose a series of puzzles which had some relevance to my kind of 'spatial' thinking. This book is the result of their work.

The puzzles are vivid, visual, varied and of course challenging. Grading puzzles in terms of degree of difficulty is always somewhat arbitrary. Given the same intelligence, what one mind finds relatively easy, another struggles with, and vice versa. Nevertheless, the editors have done what is needed in classifying the puzzles to help the reader orientate.

Having tried my hand at many of the puzzles, I am convinced that there is enough meat in the book to give everyone weeks and months of highly enjoyable puzzling.

Albie Fiori has done a magnificent job and the contribution by László Mérö of a few exceptional puzzles, which are of the professional world championship class, has added further distinction to the first Rubik Puzzle Book.

ERNO RUBIK

Which one of the figures below completes the set above?

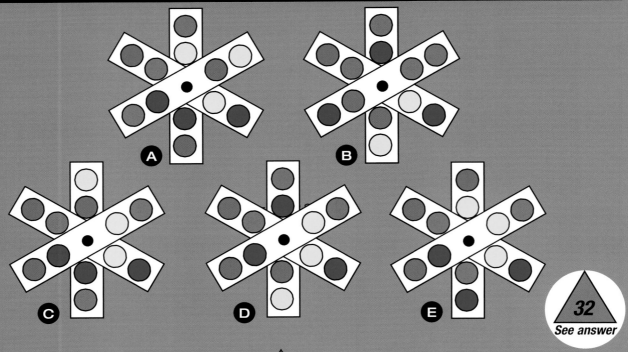

A

B

C

D

E

32
See answer

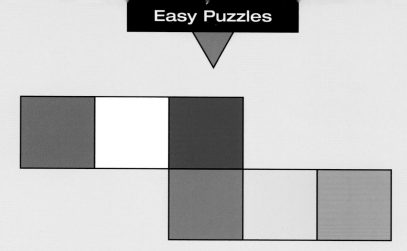

The above pattern is folded into a cube. Which one of the views below cannot be that cube?

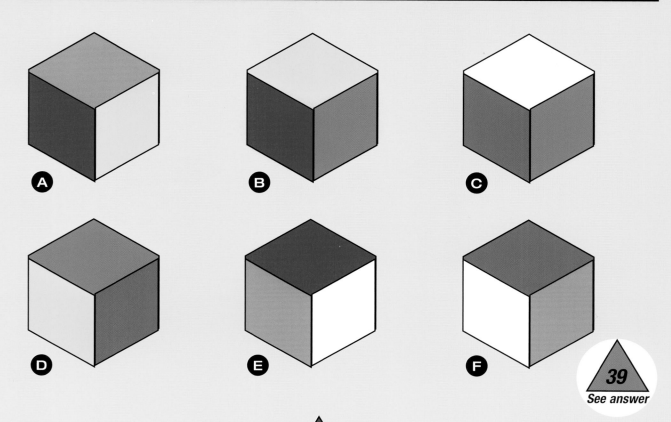

39
See answer

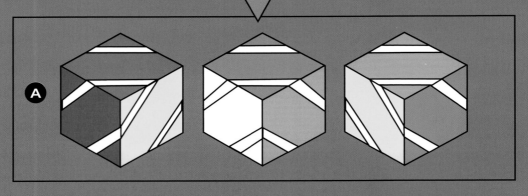

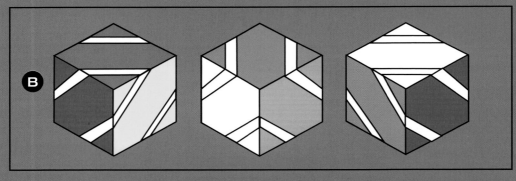

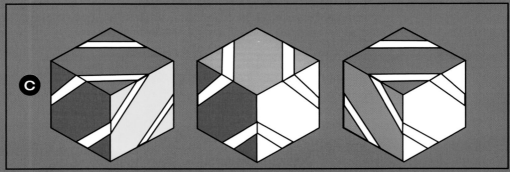

How many separate White loops on each of the three cubes?

92
See answer

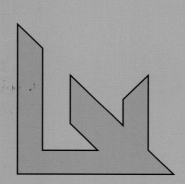

Which two pieces fit together to make a square?

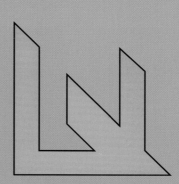

70
See answer

Which of the goblets below would complete the set above?

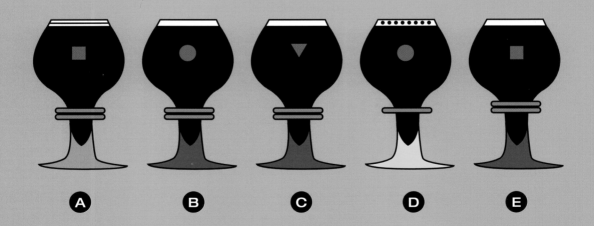

A   B   C   D   E

2
See answer

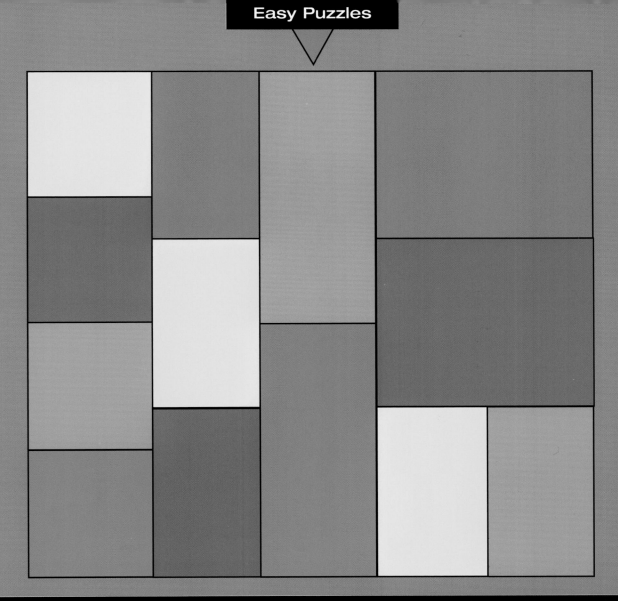

This map has been shaded so that no two areas with a common border are the same colour.
Four colours have been used. Is it possible to do the same with only three colours?

51
See answer

The tower is growing from the top down according to a simple rule. If another row were added to the bottom, how many bricks in it would be Red and how many would be Blue?

93
See answer

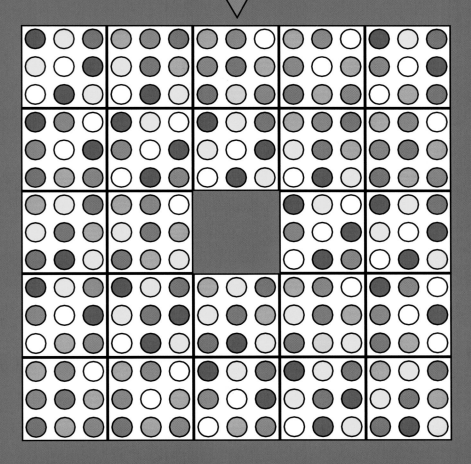

Which of the tiles below fits in the centre to match the pattern?

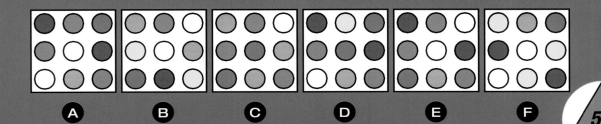

A   B   C   D   E   F

59 See answer

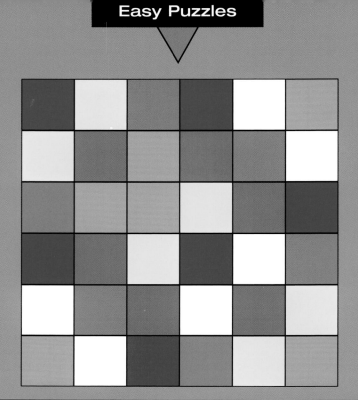

Which one of the squares below cannot be found in the mosaic above?

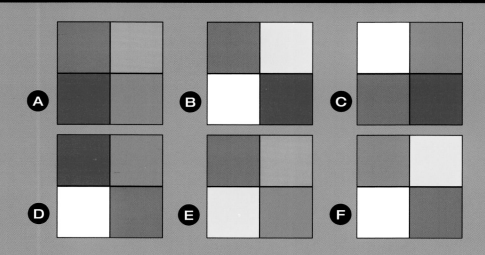

A B C

D E F

20
See answer

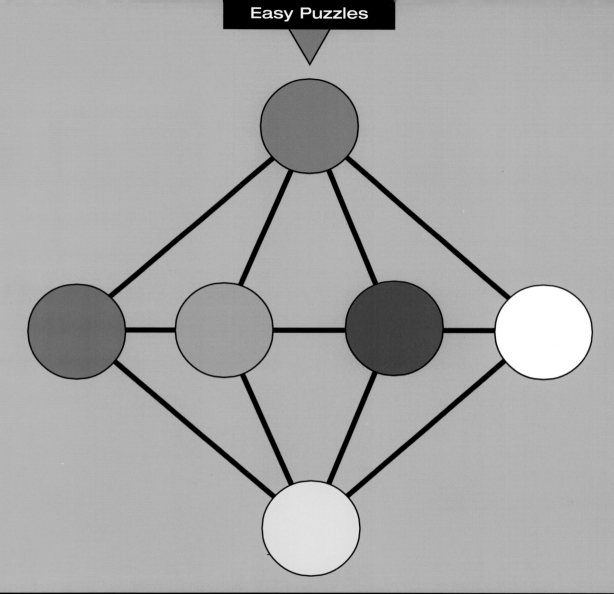

Start from one of the circles, trace a path that travels over each connecting line once only. A circle may be visited more than once. You must end in the White circle. Where must you start?

38
See answer

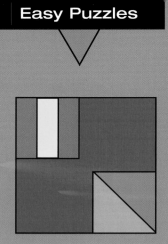

Which one of the figures below is a rotation of the figure above?

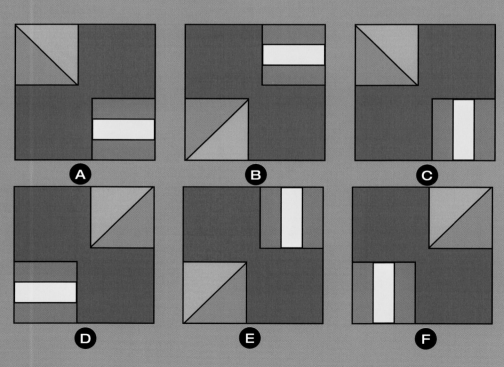

90
See answer

18

Can you spot five differences between the pictures?

67
See answer

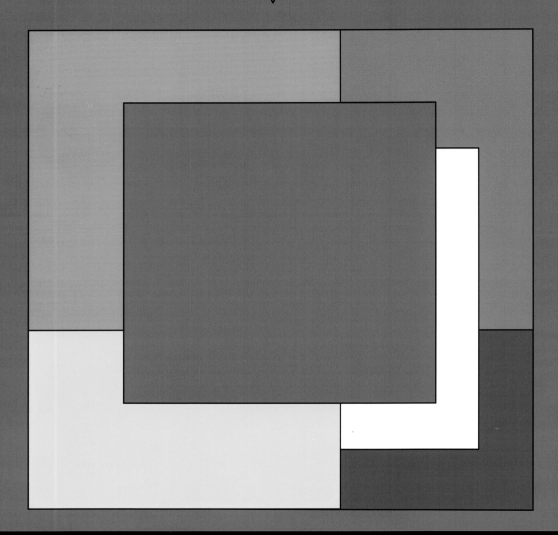

Six squares the same size have been placed one on top of the other.
In what order were they placed?

18
See answer

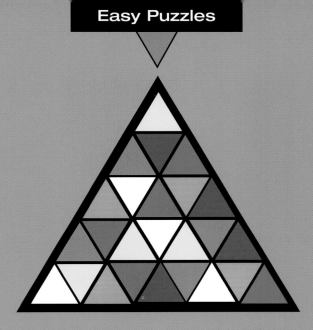

Which of the pieces below cannot be cut from the board above?

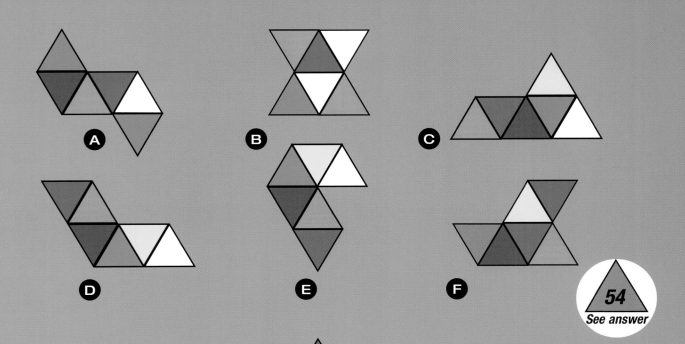

A

B

C

D

E

F

54
See answer

21

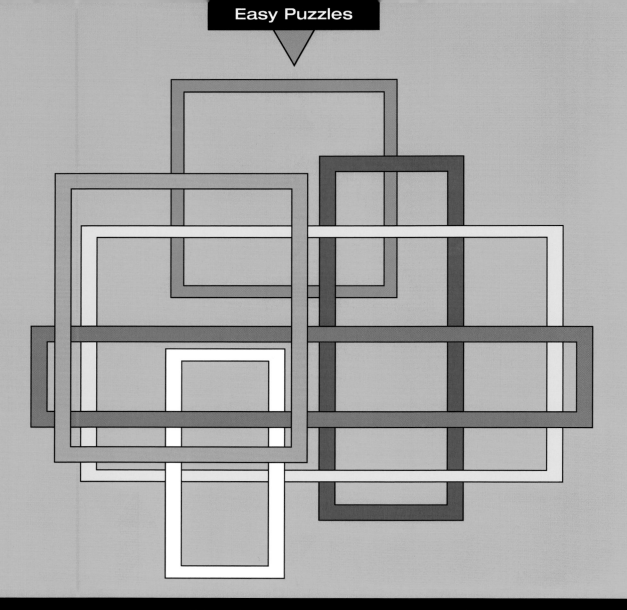

Which frame is furthest away?

82
See answer

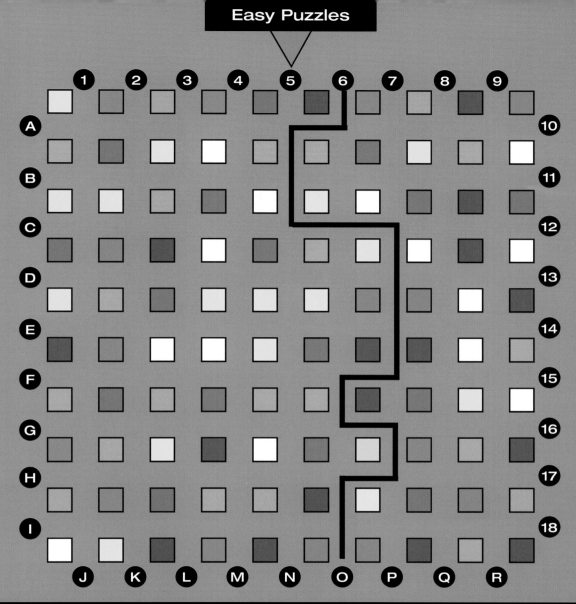

Starting from O, a path has been drawn through the grid according to certain rules.
If another path were drawn to the same rules starting from B, where would it come out?

101
See answer

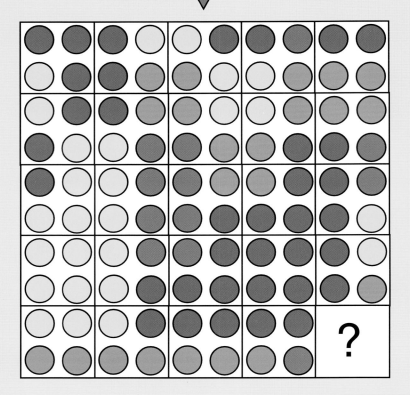

The tiles above have been laid according to a certain rule.
Which one of the tiles below can fill the last place?

A

B

C

D

E

F

33
See answer

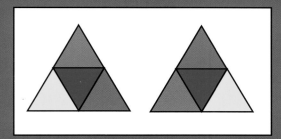
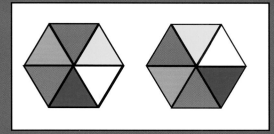

Which pair below follows the pairs above?

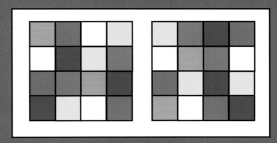

A

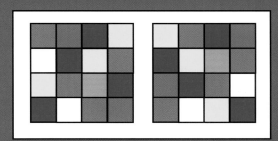

B

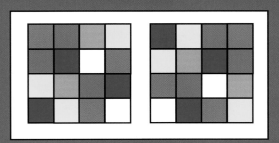

C

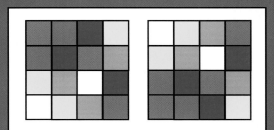

D

41
See answer

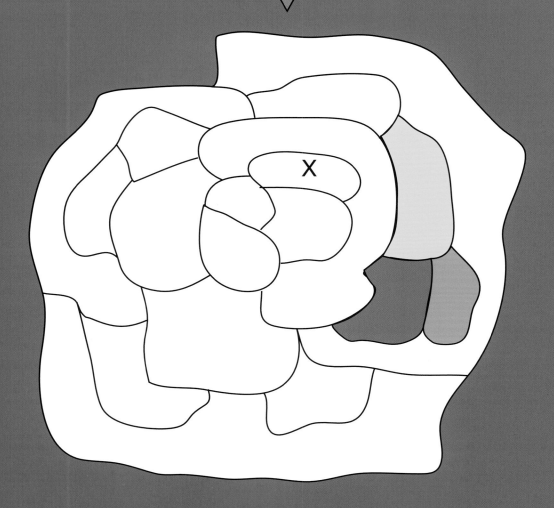

Each area of the island must be coloured Red, Yellow, Green, or Orange. No two areas with a common boundary can be of the same colour. Three areas have already been coloured. What colour will X be?

62
See answer

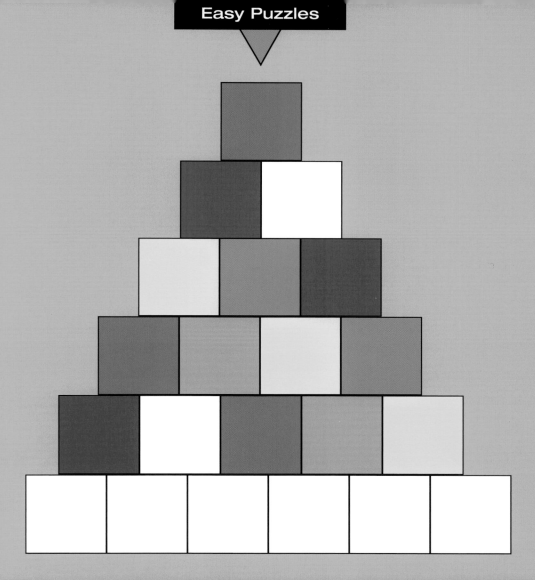

The pyramid is coloured according to a set of rules. From left to right, what colours should the bottom row be?

12
See answer

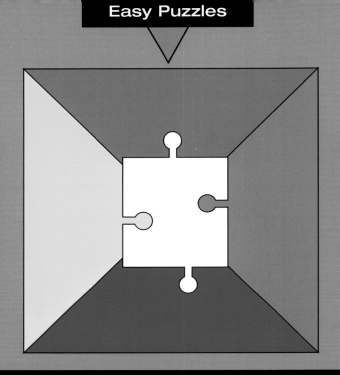

Which is the missing piece?

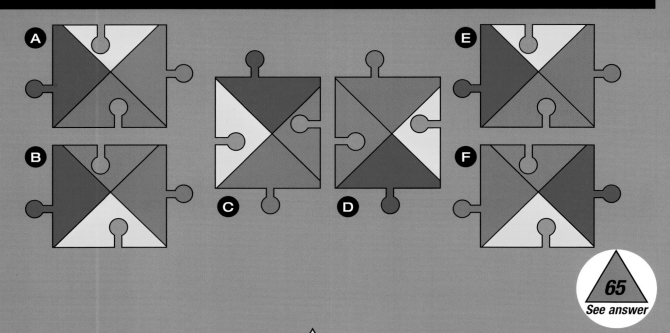

A

B

C

D

E

F

65
See answer

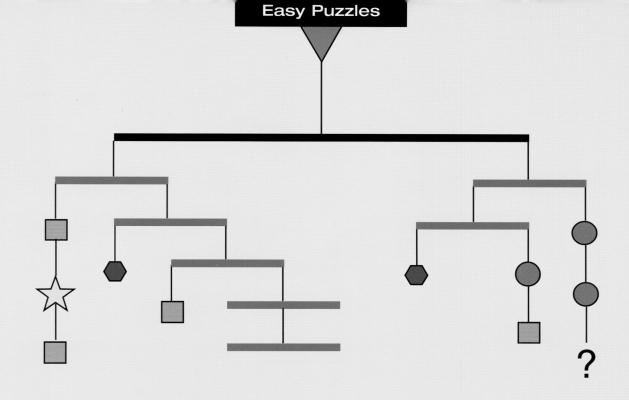

If the arrangement is to balance, what is the missing shape?

A   B   C   D   E

4
See answer

Which one of the pieces below cannot be cut from the board above?

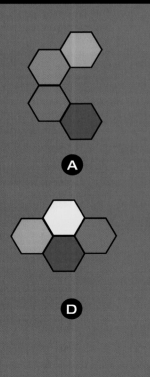

A

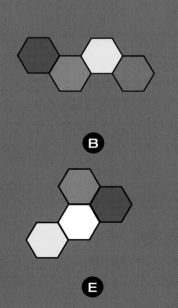

B

C

D

E

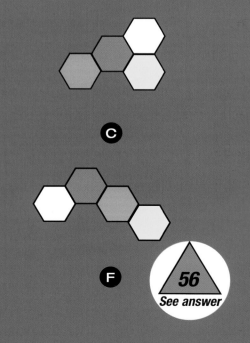

F

56
See answer

30

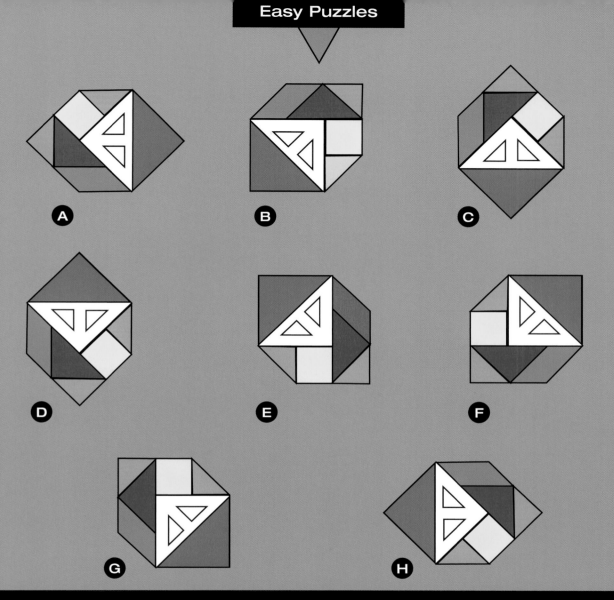

A

B

C

D

E

F

G

H

Seven are rotations of the same figure. One is a reflection. Which one?

76
See answer

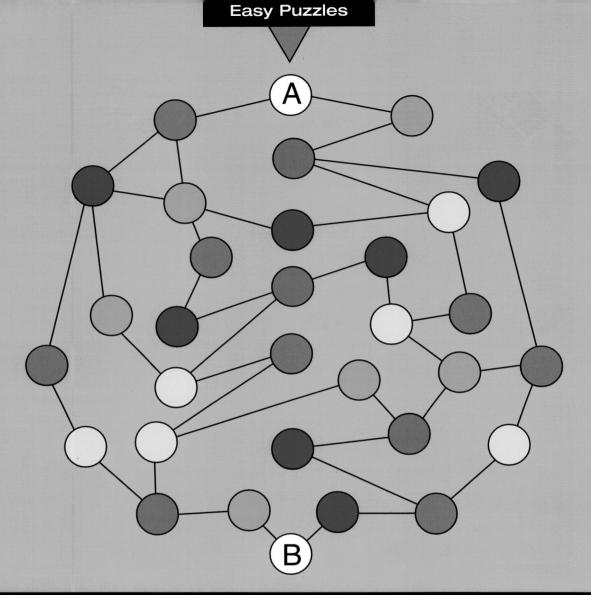

Find a path from A to B without passing through a Blue circle.
Then do the same for Yellow, Red, Orange and Green in turn.

97
See answer

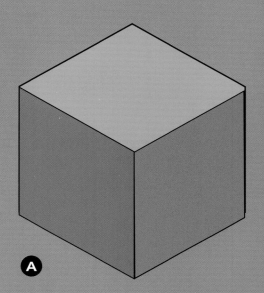

A

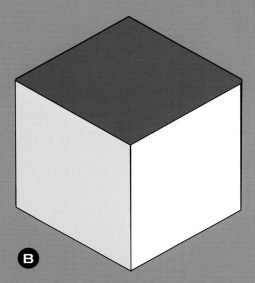

B

Which one is not a view of the same cube as the other three?

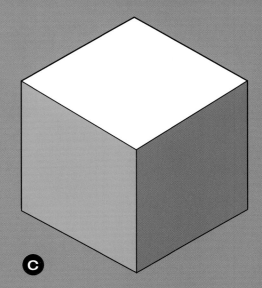

C

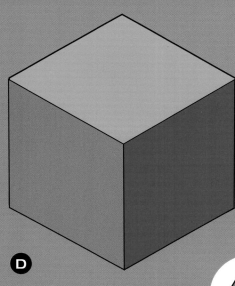

D

73
See answer

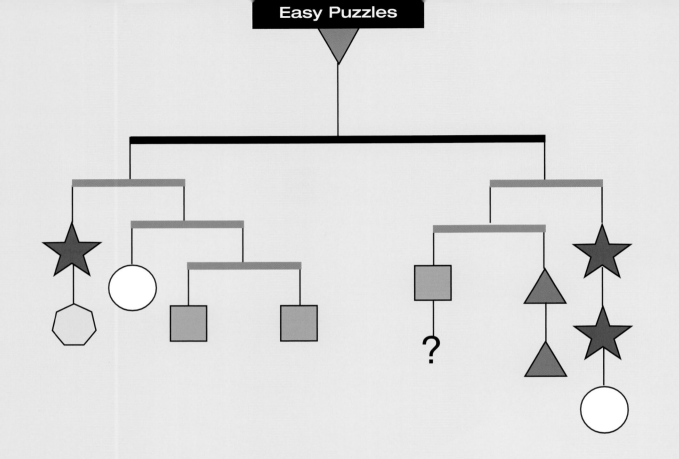

If the arrangement is to balance, what is the missing shape?

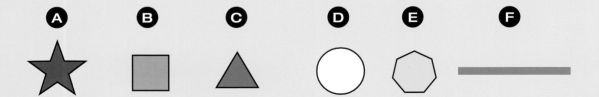

A   B   C   D   E   F

37
See answer

34

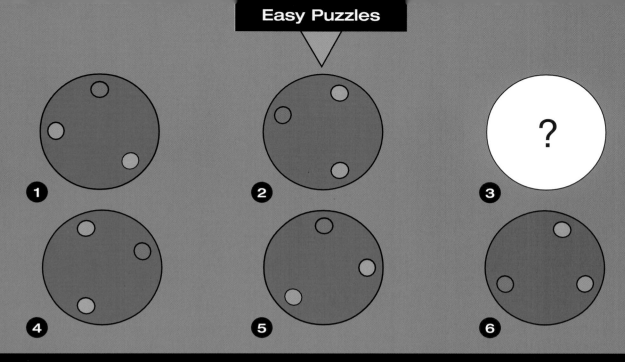

Which one of the figures below is missing from the sequence above?

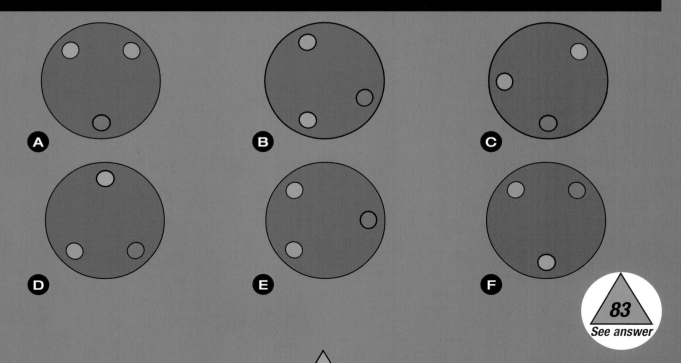

83
See answer

Which of the triangles below completes the set above?

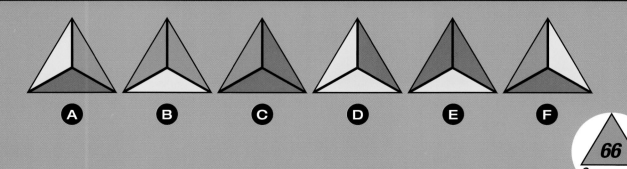

A B C D E F

66
See answer

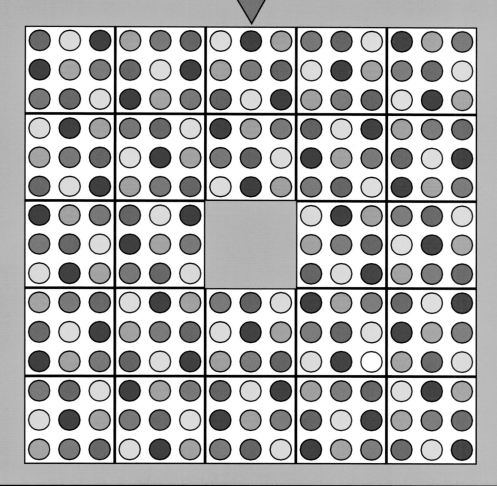

Which of the tiles below would fit in the centre to match the pattern?

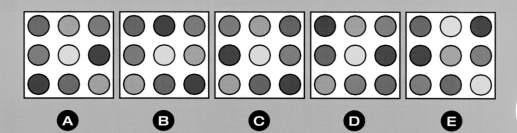

A   B   C   D   E

16
See answer

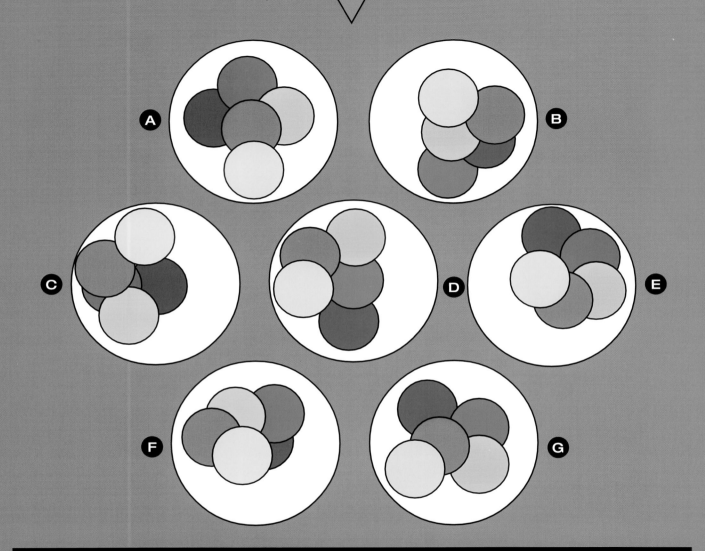

Which is the odd one out?

49
See answer

The treasure is in here.

The treasure is not in the green chest.

The treasure is not in here.

At least one of the statements on the chests is false.
Which chest contains the treasure?

5

See answer

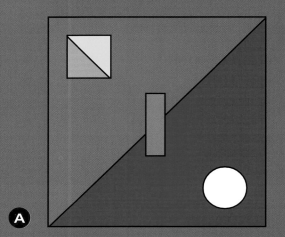
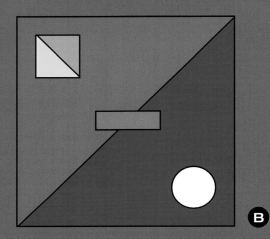

One of the images is a reflection of one of the others. The reflection may be horizontal, vertical or diagonal. Which two make the mirrored pair?

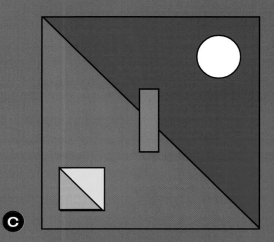
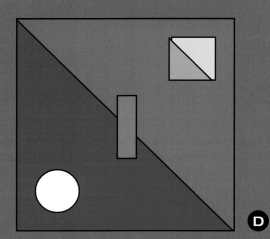

80
See answer

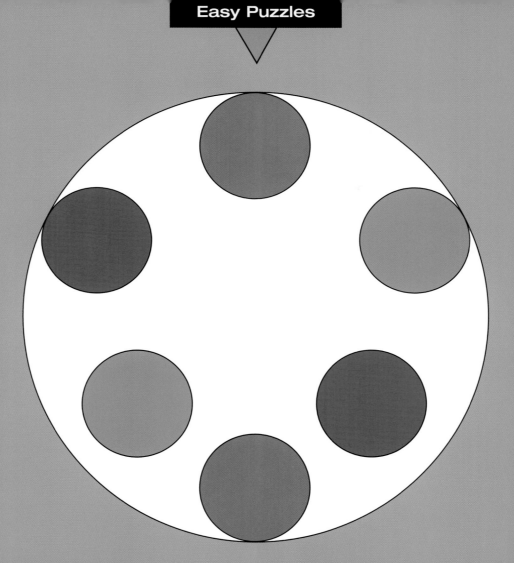

Can you connect the circles of the same colour without going outside the large circle and without the connections crossing?

98
See answer

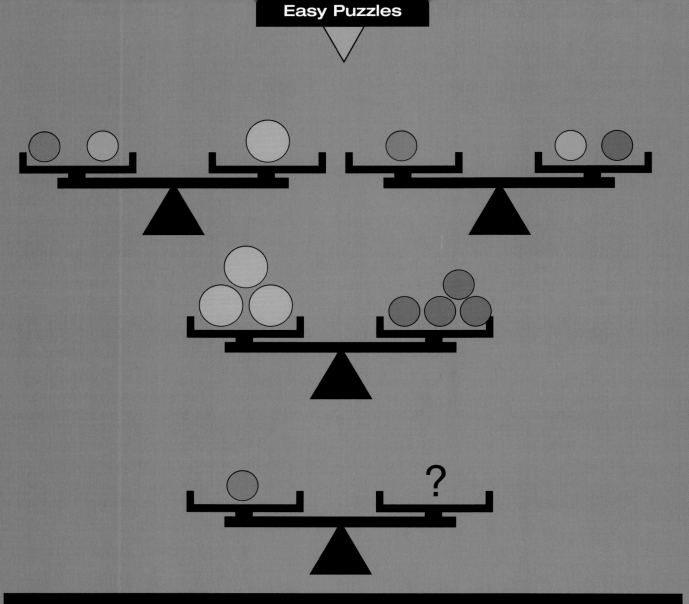

How many Green balls must be placed on the right scale pan to balance?

45
See answer

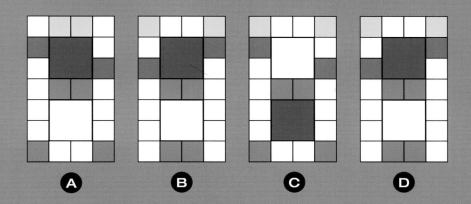

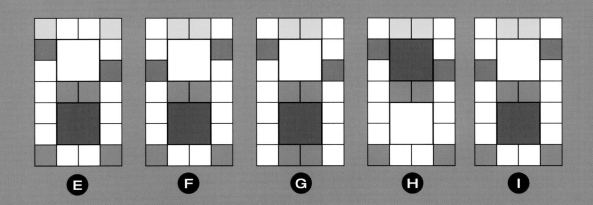

Which is the odd one out?

89
See answer

43

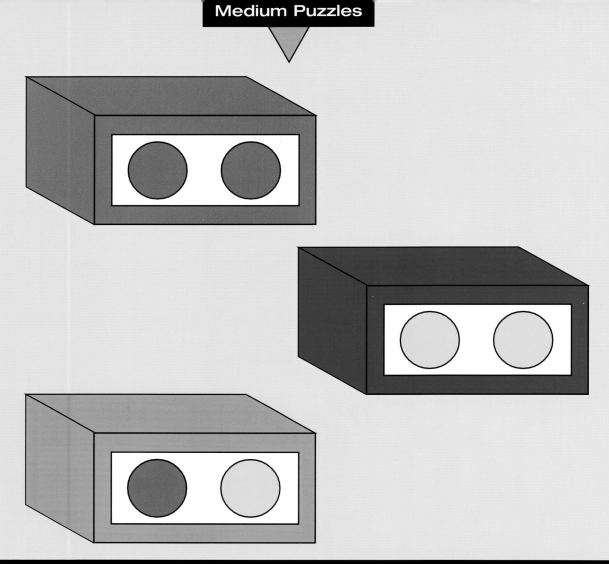

The boxes contain a total of 3 Red balls and 3 Yellow balls. There are two balls in each box. Each box has the wrong label on it. You are allowed to look at one ball taken at random from a chosen box to work out what balls are in what boxes.
Which box should you choose to see a ball from?

30
See answer

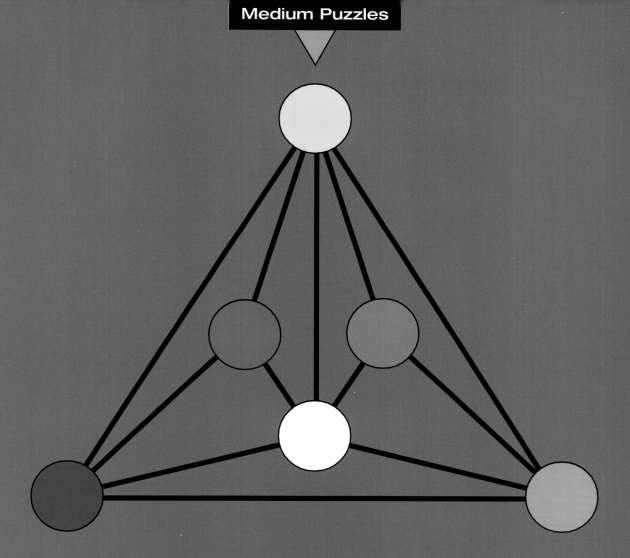

It is impossible to trace a route around the figure, from circle to circle, so that each connecting path is travelled over once only. You may add one new path, that does not cross any existing paths, so that you can trace a route starting from the Yellow circle. The path need not be a straight line. Which colour circle must be at one end of the new path?

91
See answer

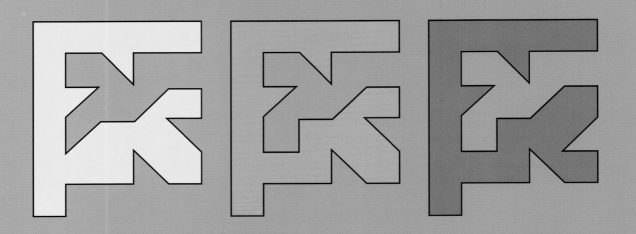

Which two pieces fit together to make a square?

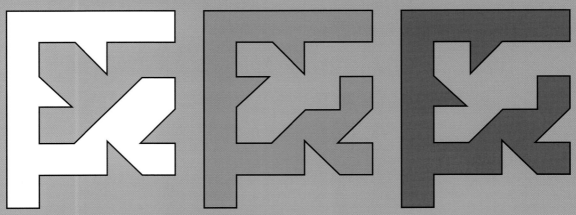

69
See answer

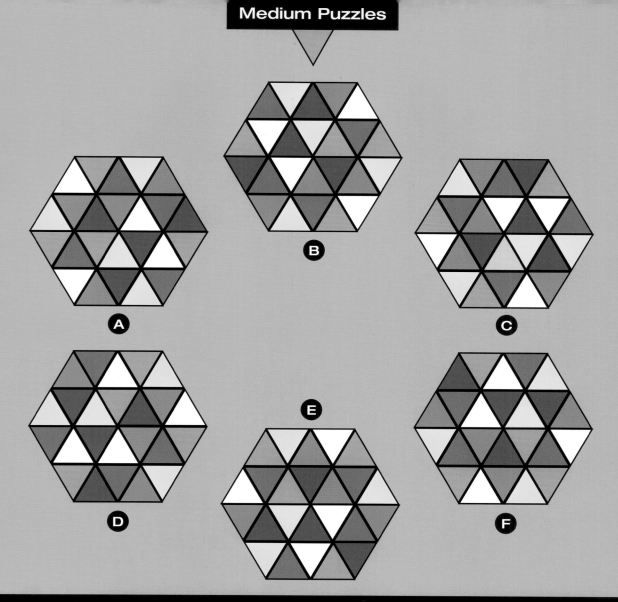

A

B

C

D

E

F

Which is the odd one out?

9
See answer

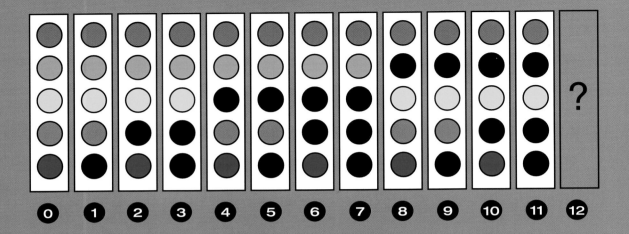

Which of the figures below is number 12 in the series above?

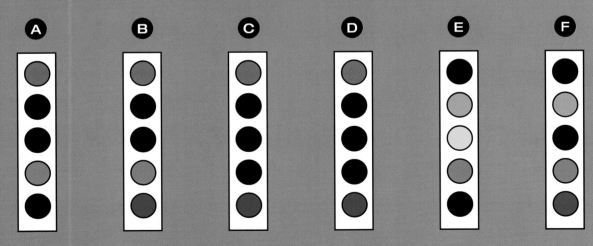

112
See answer

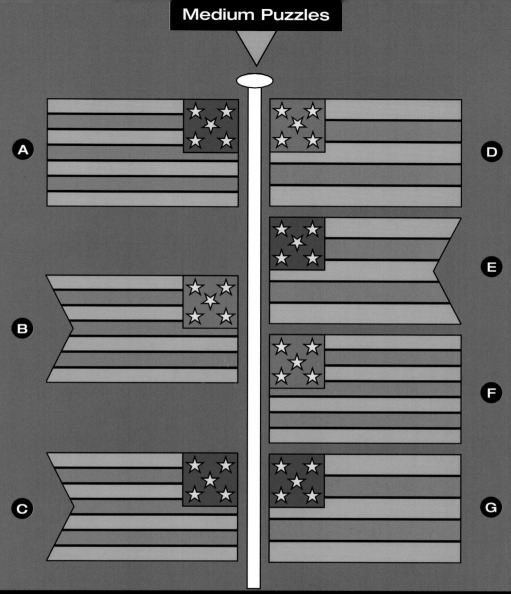

Each of the flags of the six provinces differs from the national flag in just two ways. Which is the national flag?

55
See answer

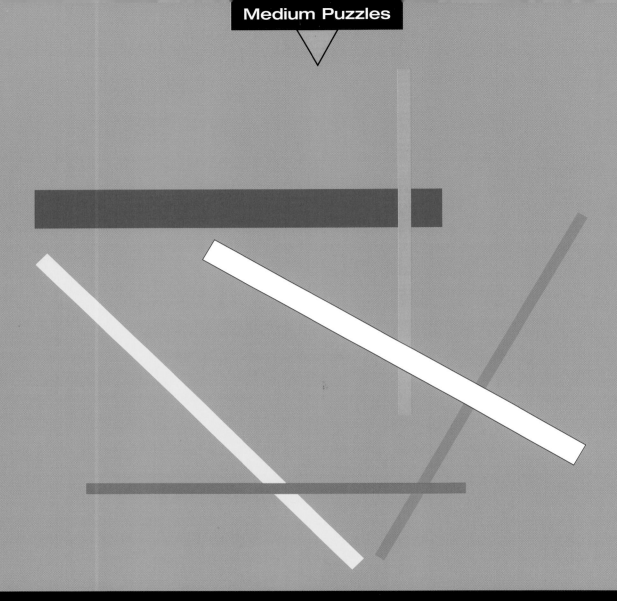

Which two lines are the same length?

105
See answer

Which one of the figures below is a mirror image of the one above?

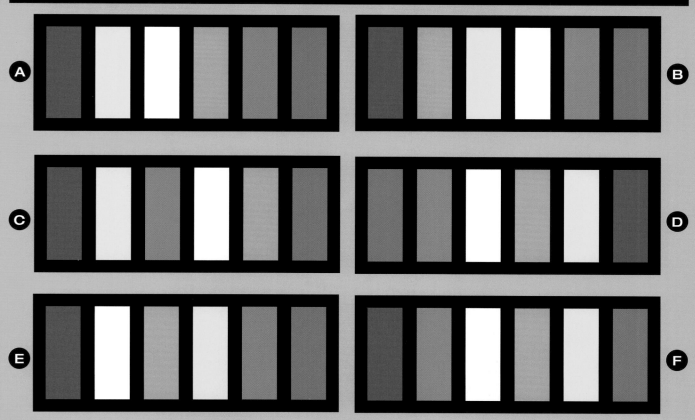

A
B
C
D
E
F

29
See answer

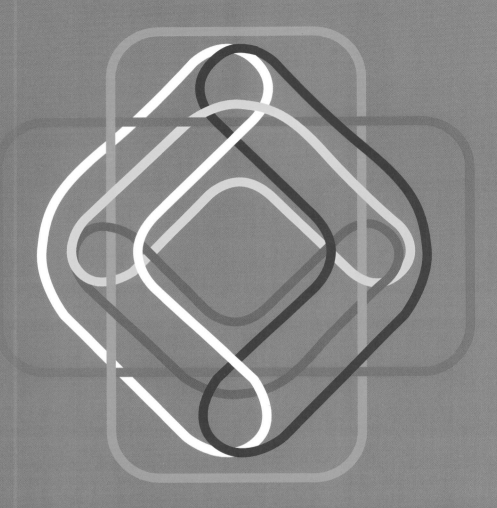

If one of the loops is cut, the others will fall loose.
Which loop should be cut?

88
See answer

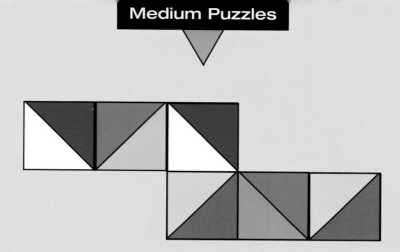

The above pattern is folded into a cube. Which one of the views below cannot be that cube?

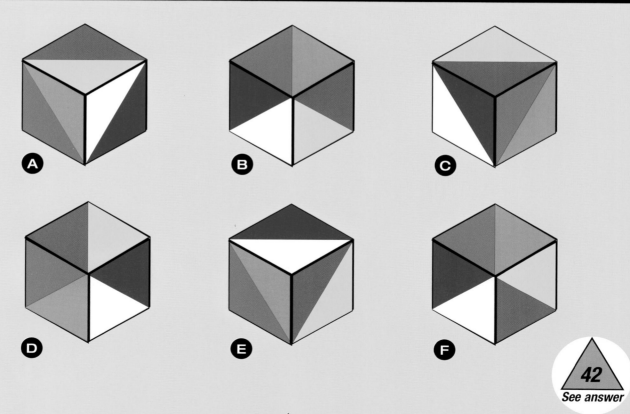

A

B

C

D

E

F

42
See answer

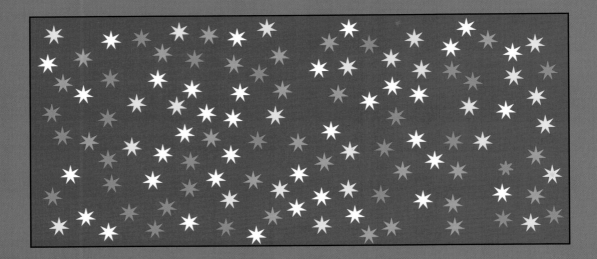

Between the two pictures, three stars have moved slightly and three others have changed colour. Can you spot all six?

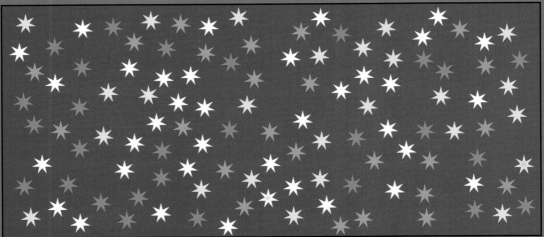

68
See answer

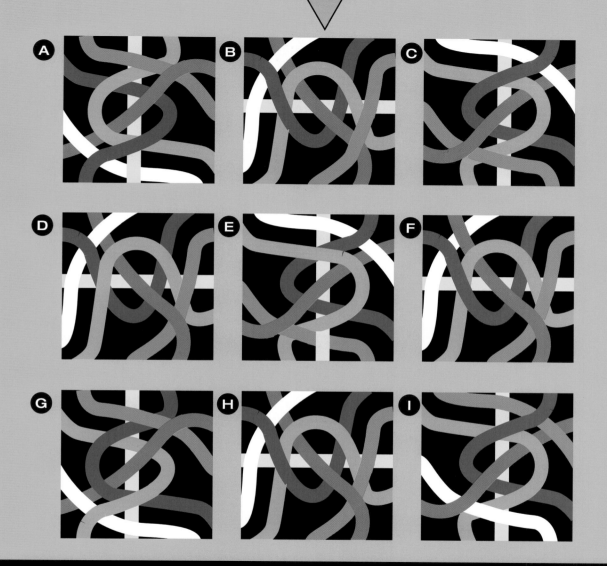

Which two tiles are the same?

50
See answer

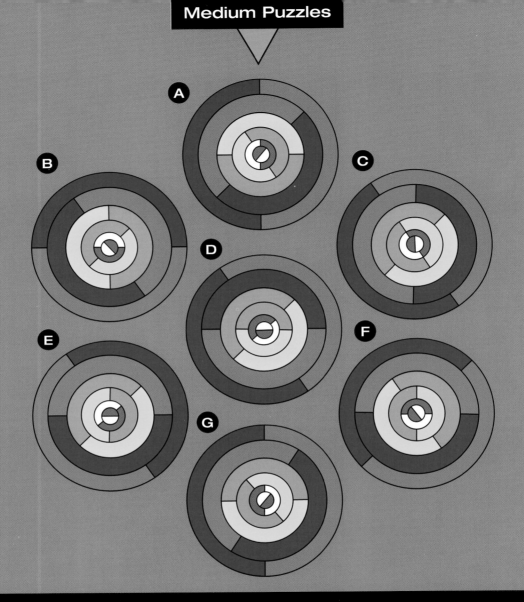

Which two wheels are the same?

14
See answer

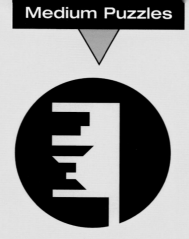

Which key fits the lock?

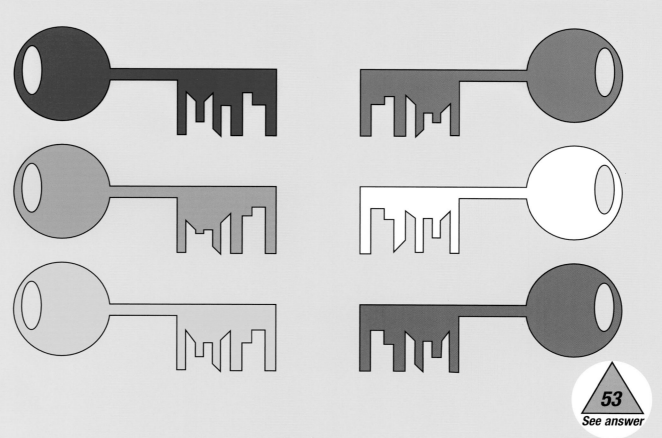

53
See answer

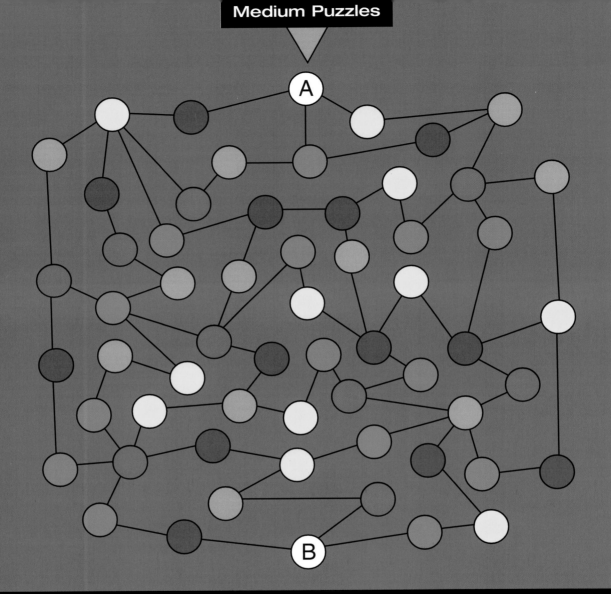

Find a path from A to B without passing through a Red circle. Then do the same for Blue, Orange, Green and Yellow in turn.

104
See answer

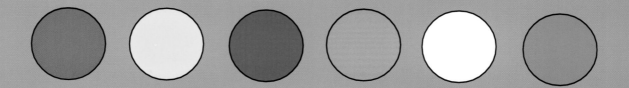

Green is not far right.
Red is between two others.
White is immediately to the left of Orange.
Yellow lies between Red and White but is adjacent to neither.
What order should the balls be in?

36
See answer

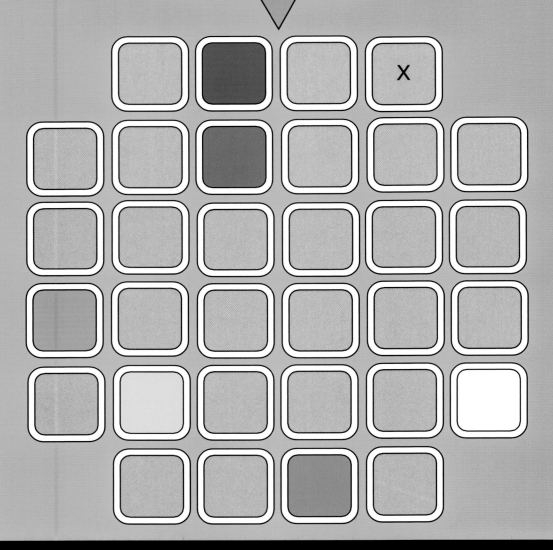

32 Yellow, Blue, Red, Orange, White and Green tiles have been placed face down on a 6x6 board above. No colour appears more than once in any column, row or diagonal line of the board. Six have been revealed. If tile X were turned over, what colour would it be?

25
See answer

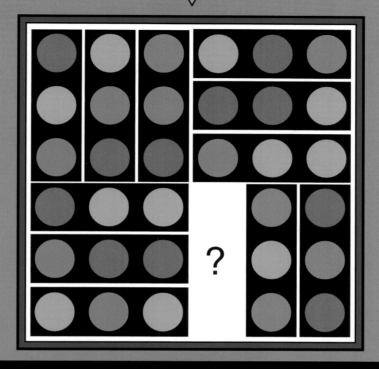

Which one of the tiles below completes the pattern above?

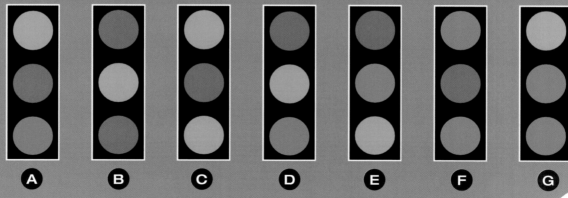

A   B   C   D   E   F   G

79
See answer

One of the strings will tighten into a knot when the ends are pulled. The others will fall apart.
Which is the knot?

94
See answer

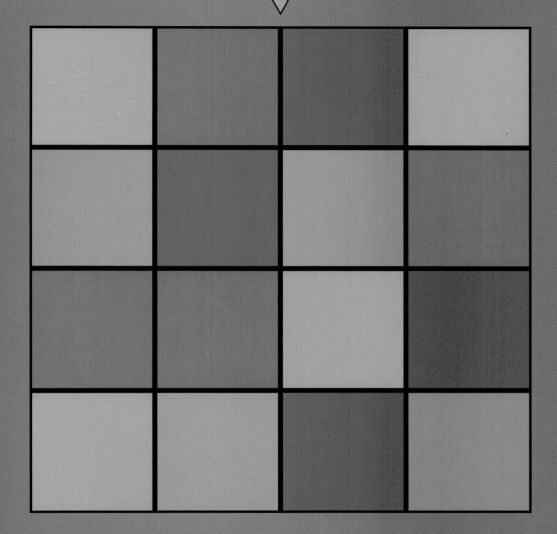

How can the square be divided into four pieces, each the same size and shape, so that each piece contains one square of each colour?

44
See answer

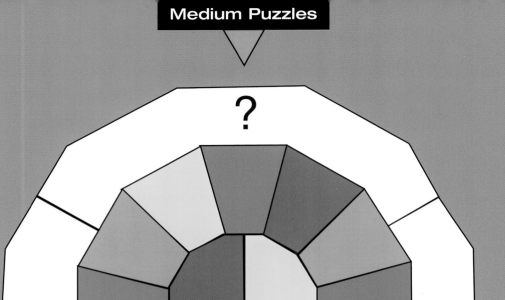

This map was being coloured so that no two areas with a common boundary were of the same colour. However, the outer areas could not be any of the colours already used. Since all maps can be coloured using only four colours, something was wrong. How should the map have been done?

74
See answer

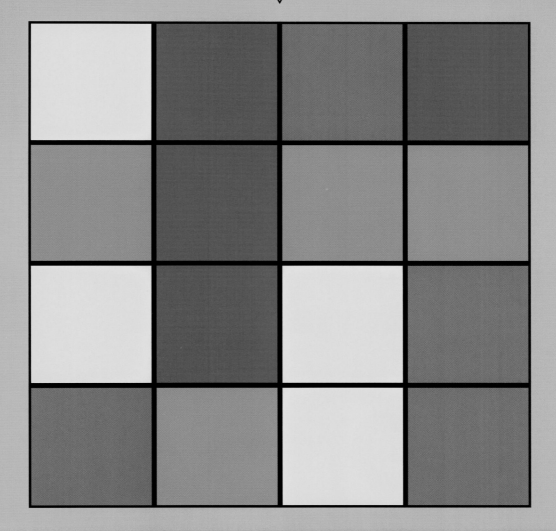

How can the square be divided into four pieces, each the same size and shape, so that each piece contains one square of each colour?

11
See answer

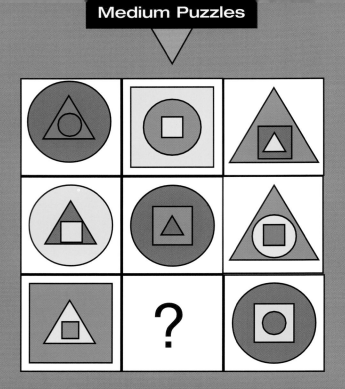

Which of the figures below completes the grid above?

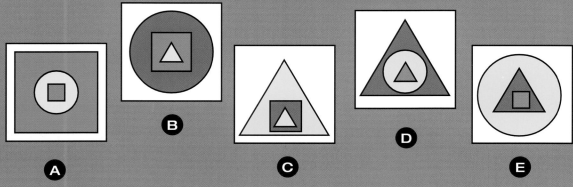

A

B

C

D

E

111
See answer

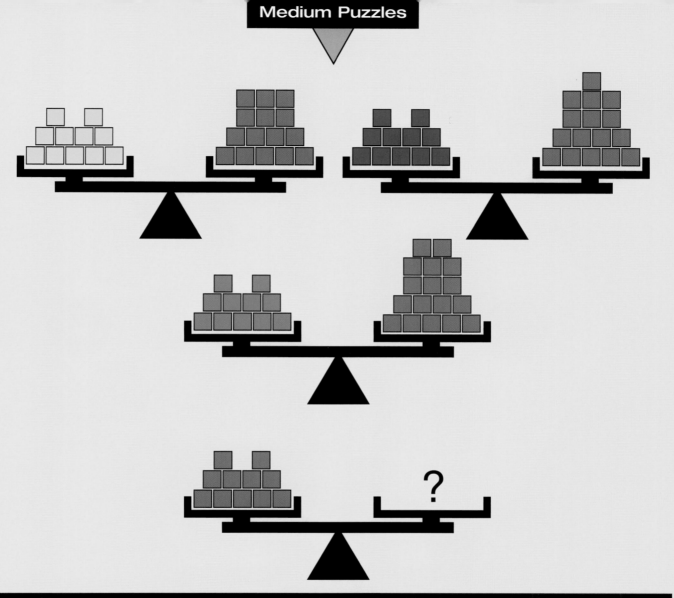

What combination of Yellow, Green, and Blue blocks will balance the Red blocks on the bottom scales?

23
See answer

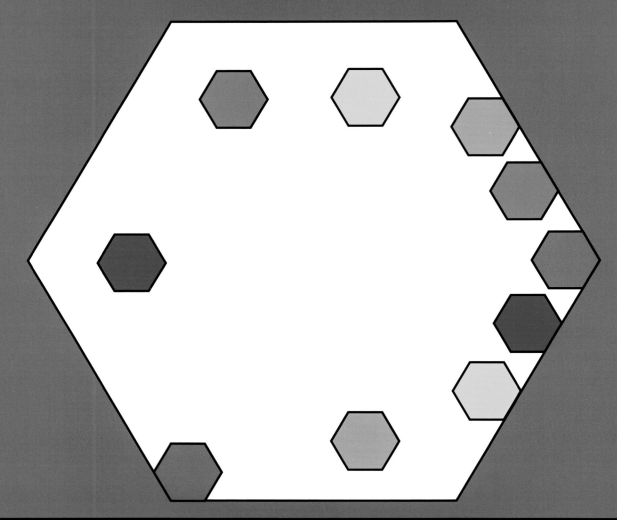

Can you connect the hexagons of the same colour without going outside the large hexagon and without the connections crossing?

99
See answer

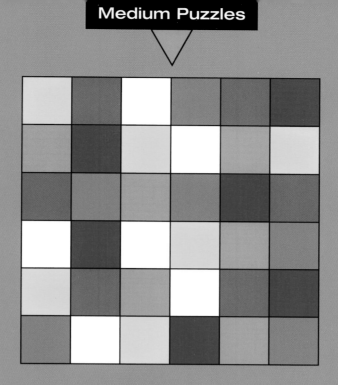

Which of the pieces below cannot be cut from the board above?

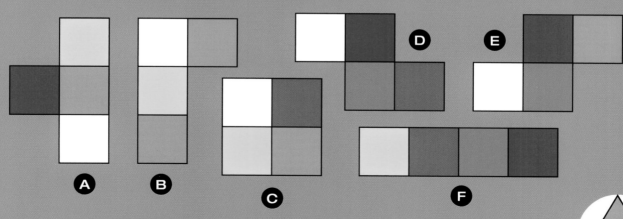

A

B

C

D

E

F

27
See answer

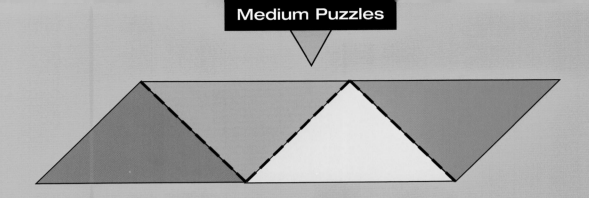

Each triangle is the same colour on the other side. The strip can be folded along the dotted lines in various ways to make a square with a different colour pattern on each side. Which one of the squares below cannot be made?

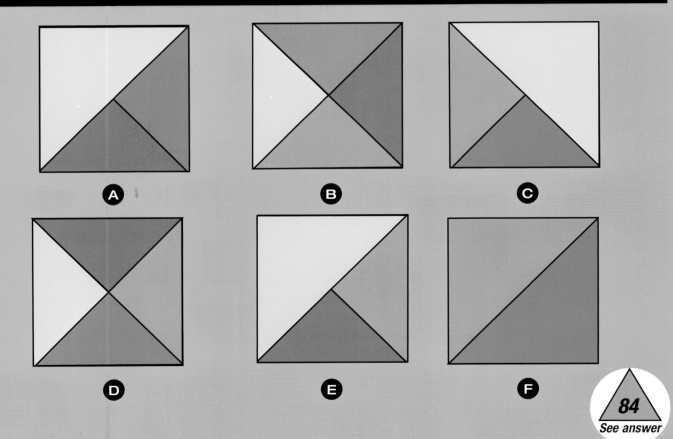

A

B

C

D

E

F

84
See answer

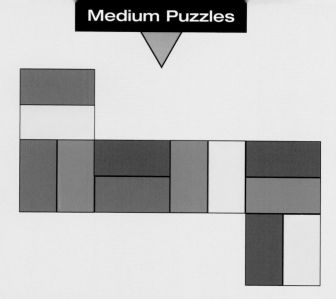

The above pattern is folded into a cube.
Which one of the views below cannot be that cube?

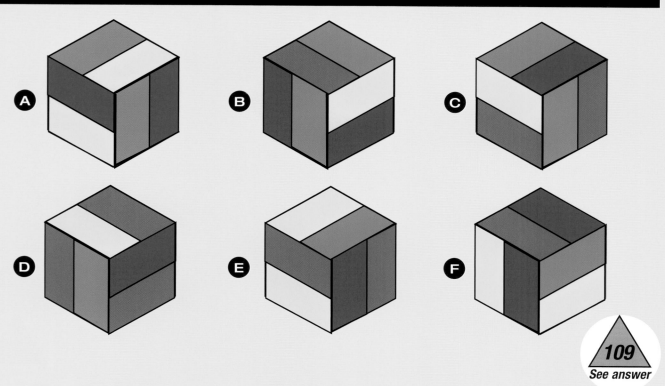

A B C

D E F

109
See answer

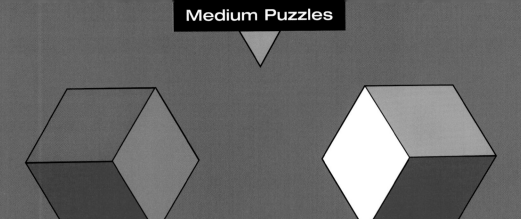

Above are two views of a cube. The unseen face is yellow.
Which of the views below could be of the same cube?

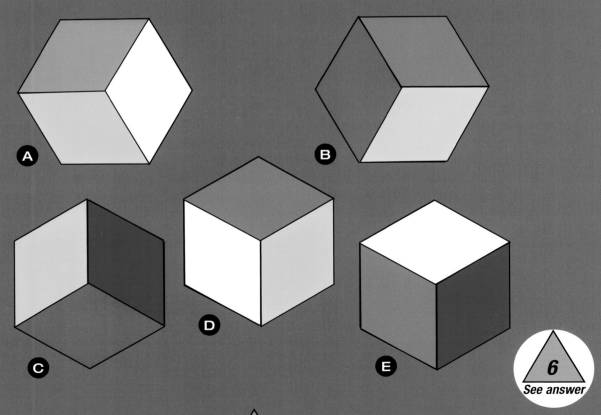

A
B
C
D
E

6
See answer

72

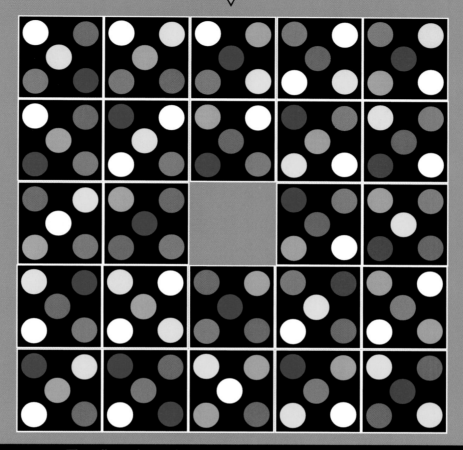

The tiles above have been laid to a certain rule.
Which of one of the tiles below must go in the space?

 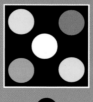 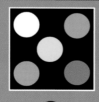

A   **B**   **C**   **D**   **E**   **F**

47
See answer

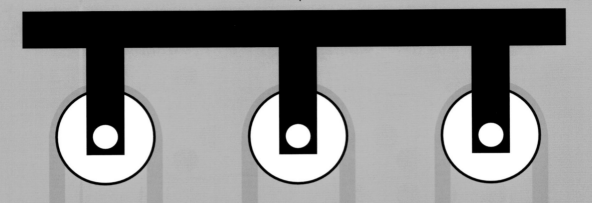

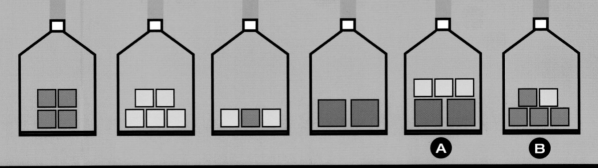

The first two pulleys are balanced. Is the third balanced or, if not, will A or B descend?

103
See answer

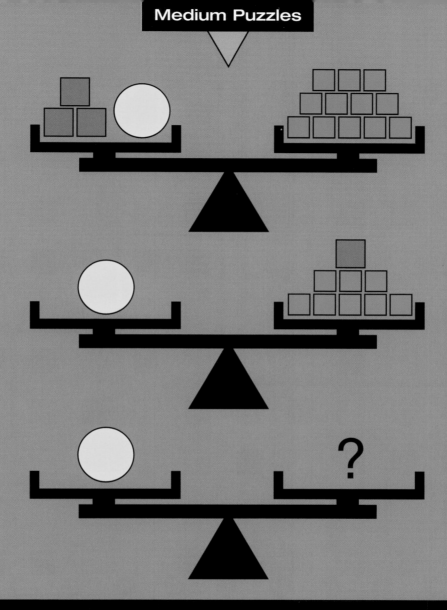

How many Green blocks are needed to balance the Yellow ball?

24
See answer

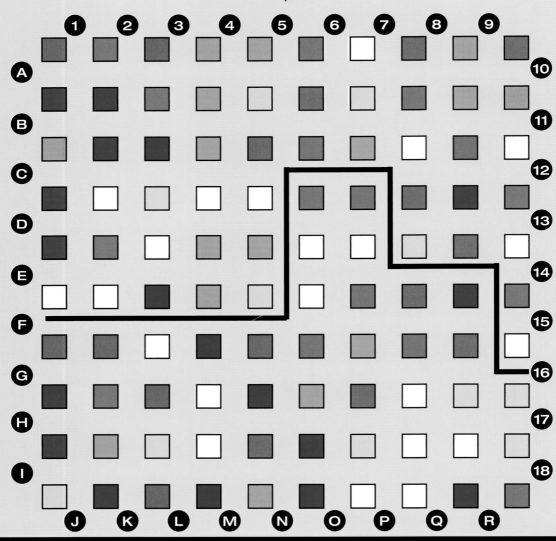

Starting from 16, a path has been drawn through the grid according to certain rules.
If another path were drawn to the same rules starting from 14, where would it come out?

100
See answer

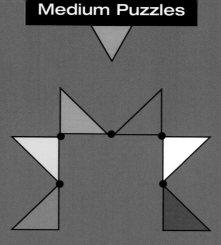

The triangles are hinged at the corners as shown to form a chain.
The chain may cross itself. Which of the figures below cannot be formed?

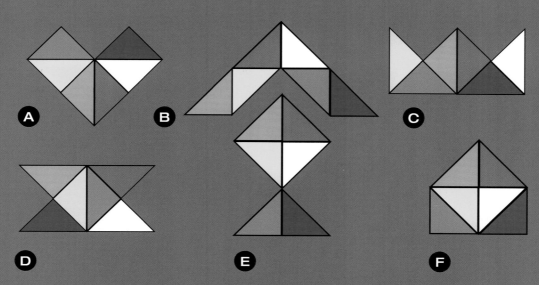

A

B

C

D

E

F

87
See answer

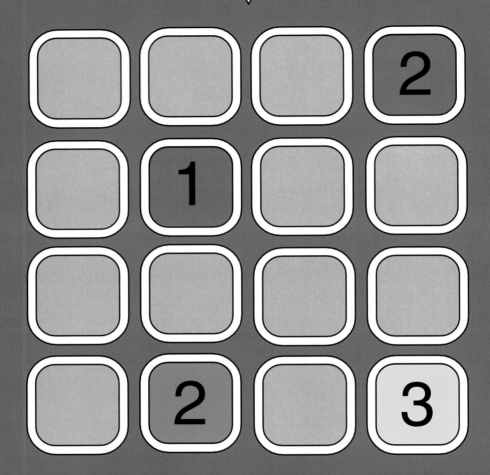

Four Red tiles numbered 1 to 4, and the same of Blue, Green and Yellow, have been placed face down above. They have been arranged so that no row, column or corner-to-corner diagonal contains two tiles of the same colour or number. Four tiles have been revealed. What is the complete layout?

34
See answer

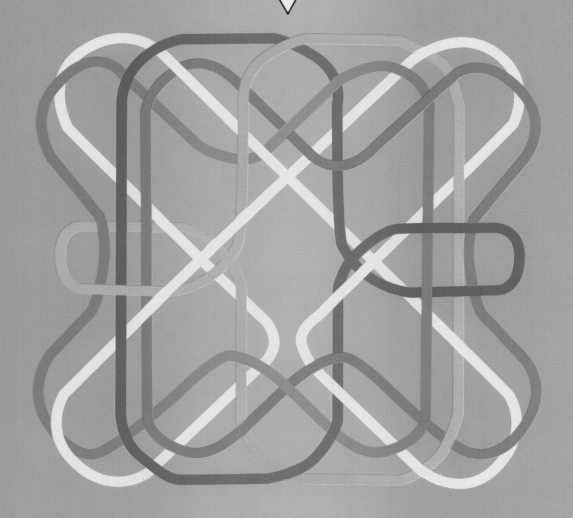

Four of the five rope loops are linked. Which colour loop can be removed without cutting?

15
See answer

Four squares have been overlapped above to create 13 different areas.
How can you overlap four squares to create 49 different areas?

52
See answer

Find a path from A to B without passing through a Red square. The do the same for Yellow,
Green, Blue and Orange in turn.

95
See answer

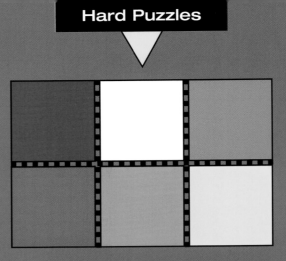

The sheet of paper above is folded along the dotted lines to make a 6 page book.
It is bound on one edge and the folds cut so the book can open.
Each page is the same colour on both sides.
Which one of the books below cannot be made?

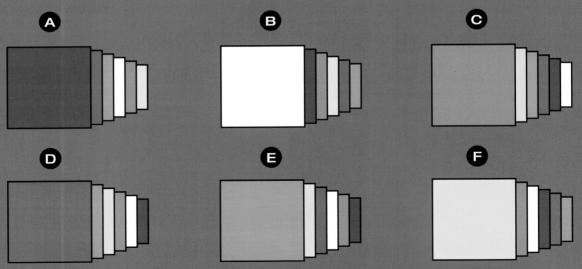

A

B

C

D

E

F

71
See answer

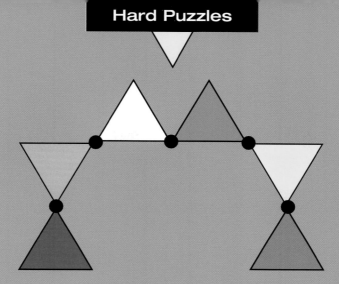

The triangles are hinged at the corners to form a chain. The chain may cross itself. Which one of the figures below cannot be formed?

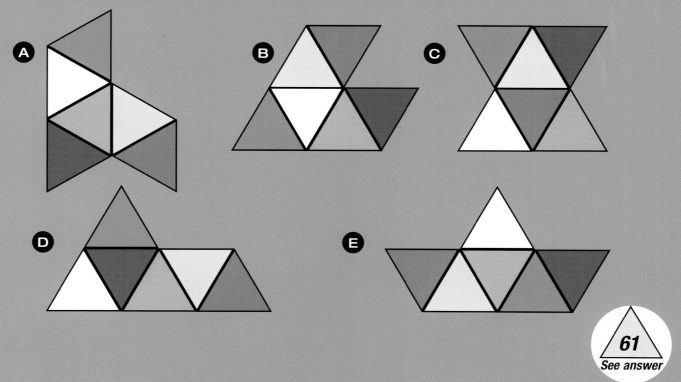

A

B

C

D

E

61
See answer

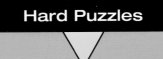

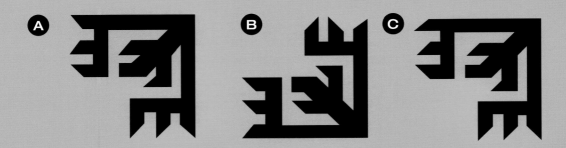

Which one of the pieces below fits in one of the holes above?

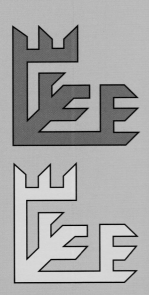

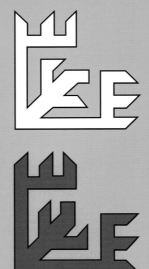

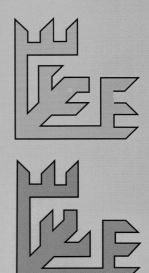

107
See answer

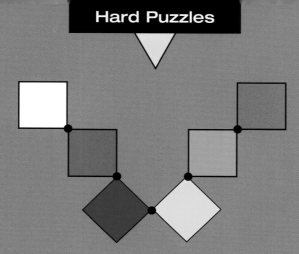

The squares are hinged at the corners as shown to form a chain. The chain may cross itself. Which one of the figures below cannot be formed?

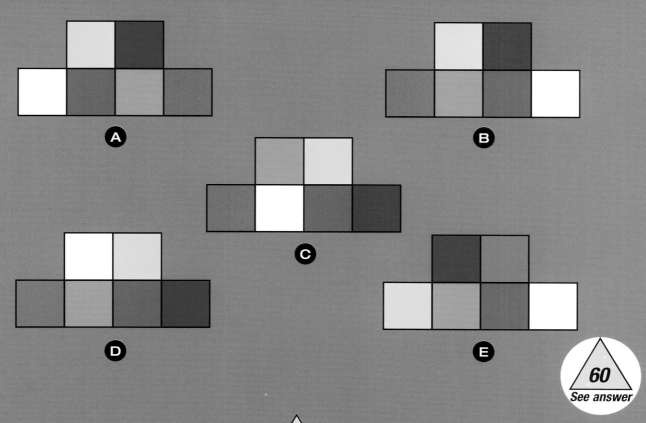

A

B

C

D

E

60
See answer

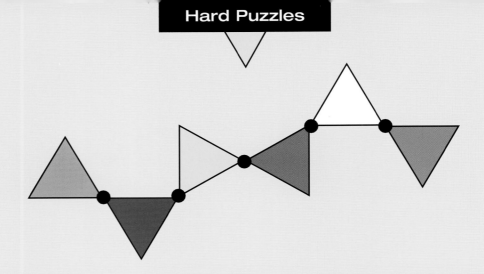

The triangles are hinged at the corners to form a chain. The chain may cross itself. Which one of the figures below cannot be formed?

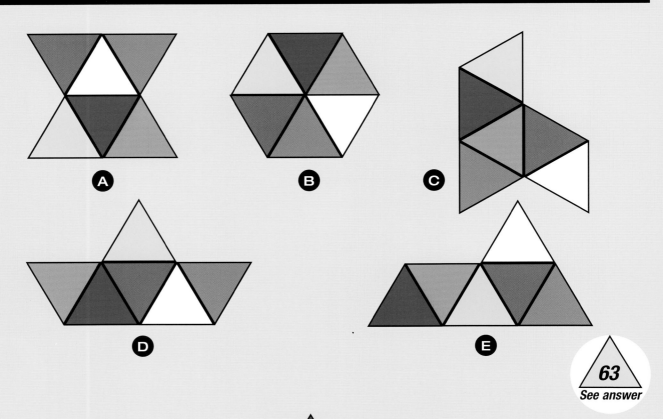

A

B

C

D

E

63
See answer

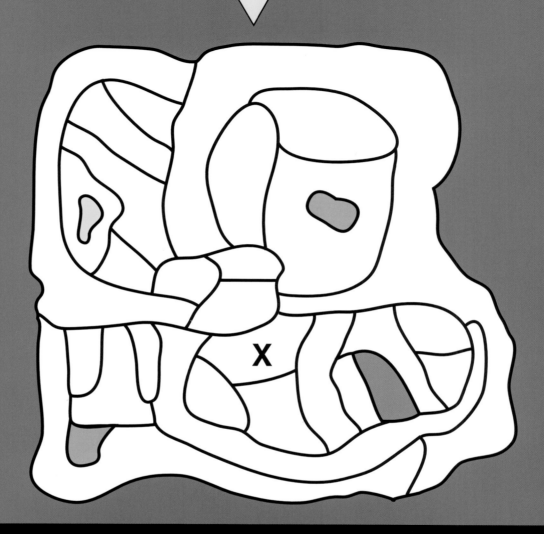

Each area of the island must be coloured Red, Yellow, Green, or Orange. No two areas with a common boundary can be of the same colour. Four areas have already been coloured. What colour will the area marked 'X' be?

13
See answer

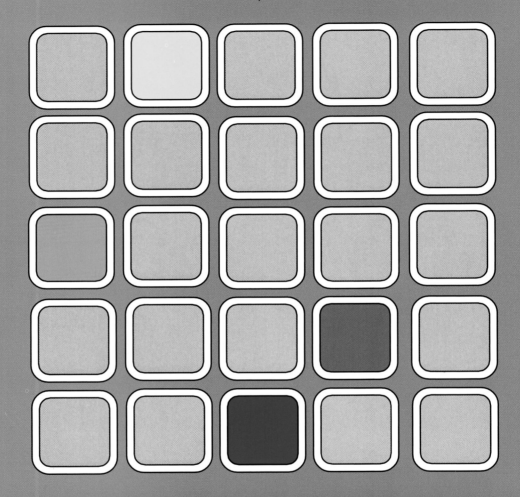

Red, Yellow Blue, Green and Orange tiles have been placed face down above. They have been arranged so that no row, column or corner-to-corner diagonal contains two tiles of the same colour. Four tiles have been revealed. What is the complete layout?

48
See answer

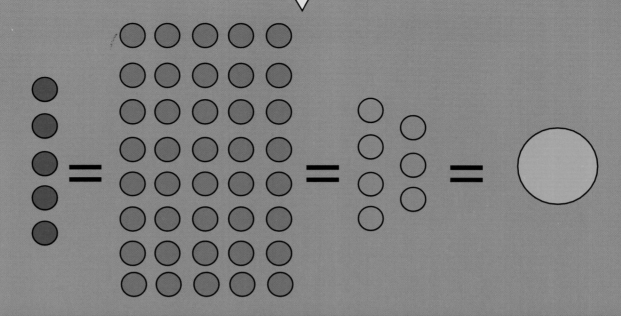

The blank coins below are Red, Blue, or Green. How many should there be of each?

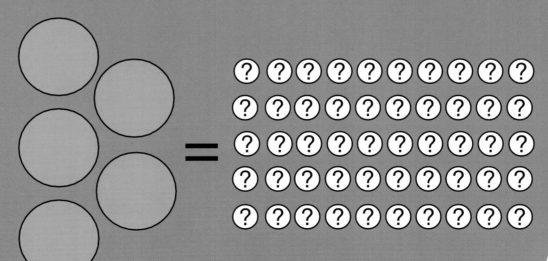

3
See answer

If there is a Red star on one side of the card, then there is a Green circle on the other side.

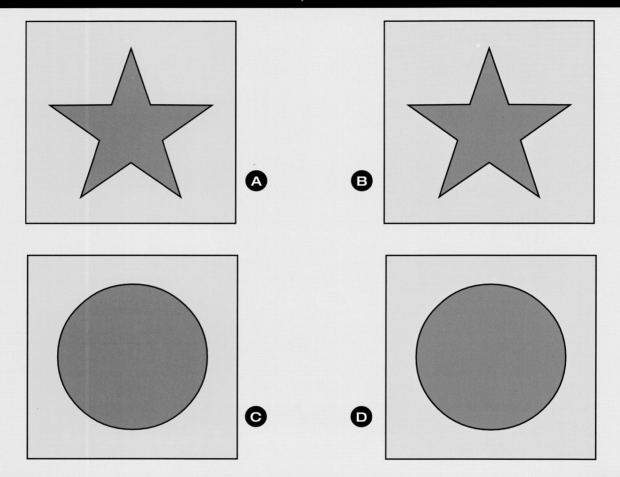

A B

C D

Each card has a star on one side and a circle on the other. All are either Red or Green. Of the four cards, which two only would need to be turned to find out if the statement at the top of the page is true or false?

86
See answer

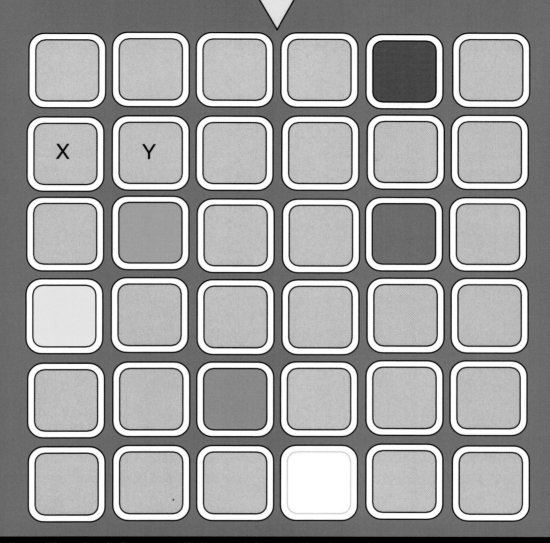

36 Yellow, Blue, Red, Orange, White and Green tiles have been placed face down above.
No two adjacent tiles, horizontally, vertically or diagonally, are the same colour.
No colour appears more than once in any column or row. Six have been revealed.
If Y is not Yellow, what colour is X?

31
See answer

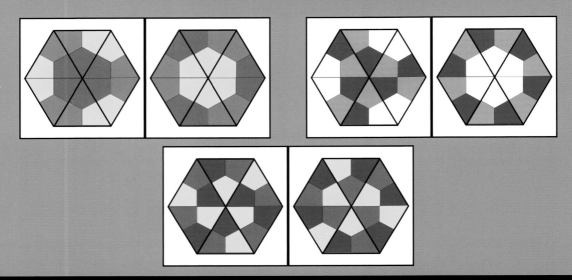

Which of the pairs below conforms with those above?

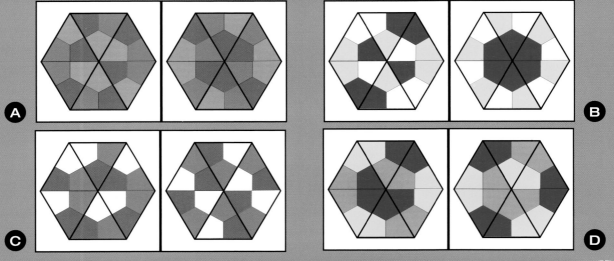

A

B

C

D

106
See answer

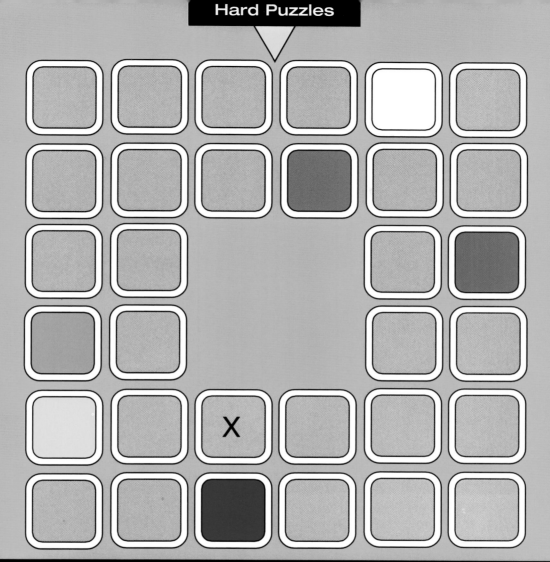

32 Yellow, Blue, Red, Orange, White and Green tiles have been placed face down on a 6x6 board above. No colour appears more than once in any column, row or diagonal line of the board. Six have been revealed. You may reveal one more tile, other than X, to help you determine what X is. Which tile should you turn?

22
See answer

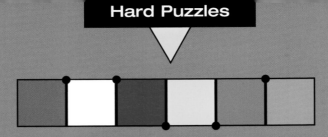

The squares are hinged at the corners as shown to form a chain. The chain may cross itself. Which one of the figures below cannot be formed?

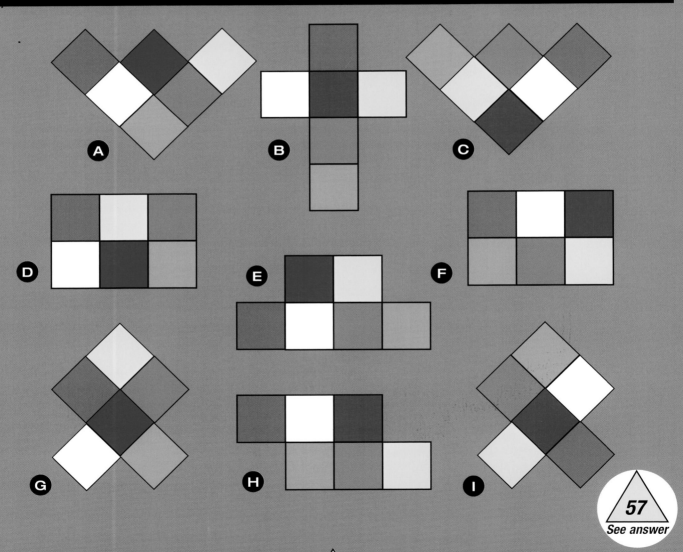

A B C

D E F

G H I

57
See answer

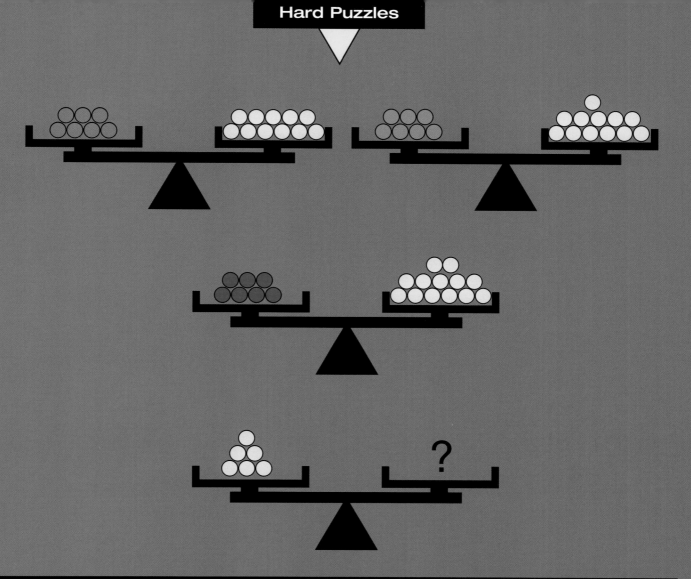

How can 6 balls, none of which may be Yellow, be added to the bottom
scales for them to balance?

26
See answer

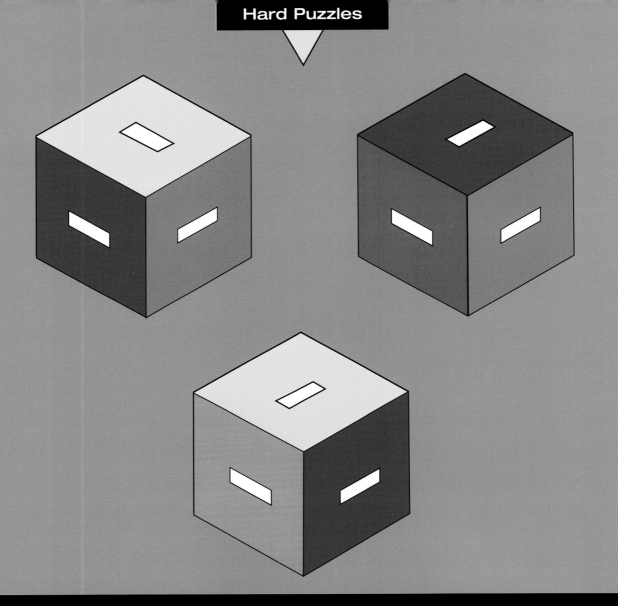

Three views of the same cube. Any unseen face is White. What colour is opposite Yellow?

77
See answer

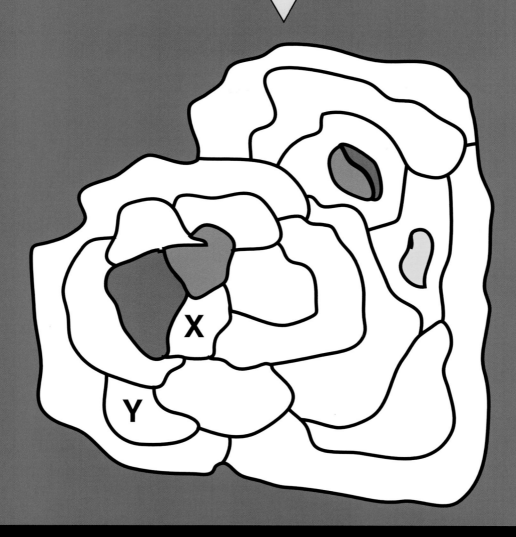

Each area of the island must be coloured Red, Yellow, Green, or Orange. No two areas with a common boundary can be of the same colour. Five areas have already been coloured. The areas marked 'X' and 'Y' are different colours. Exactly what colour is each?

21
See answer

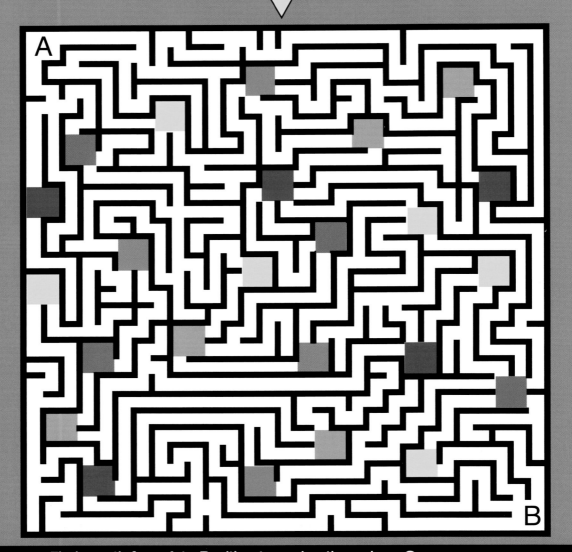

Find a path from A to B without passing through an Orange square.
Then do the same for Green, Blue, Red and Yellow in turn.

96
See answer

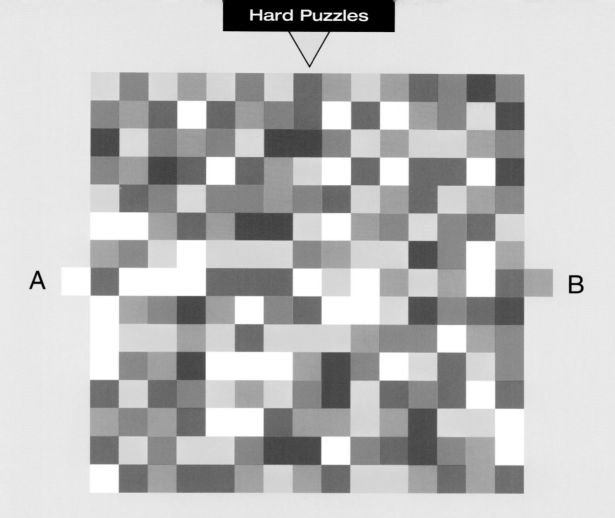

A

B

Go from A to B. No diagonal moves. You may only move from one colour to another as follows:

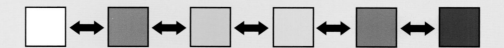

35
See answer

Each area of the island must be coloured Red, Yellow, Green, or Orange. No two areas with a common boundary can be of the same colour. Seven areas have already been coloured. What colour will X be?

64
See answer

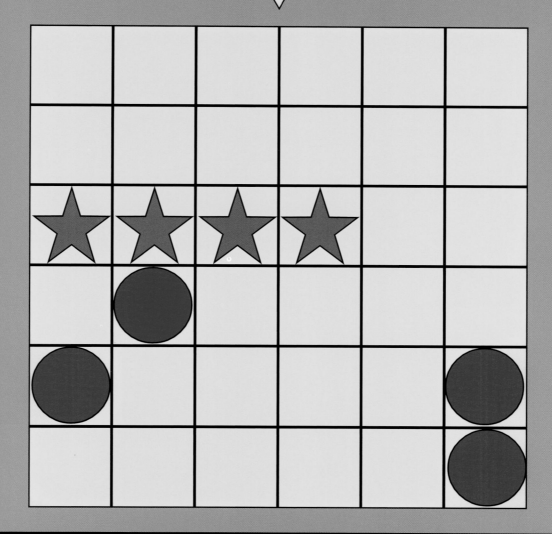

Can you divide the board into four parts along the grid lines, all the same shape and size, so that each part contains a star and a circle?

85
See answer

A

B

C

Which one of the pieces below fits in one of the holes above?

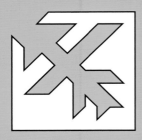

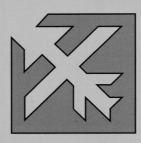

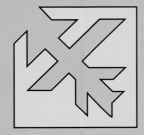

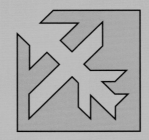

108
See answer

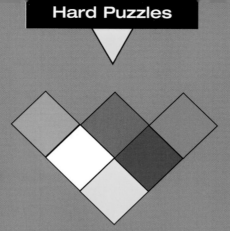

Each row of squares below is hinged at the corners as shown to form a chain.
A chain may cross itself. Which one of the chains cannot form the figure above?

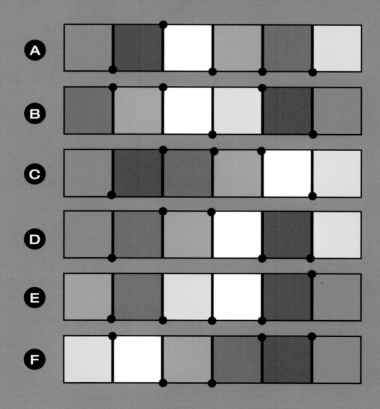

A

B

C

D

E

F

58
See answer

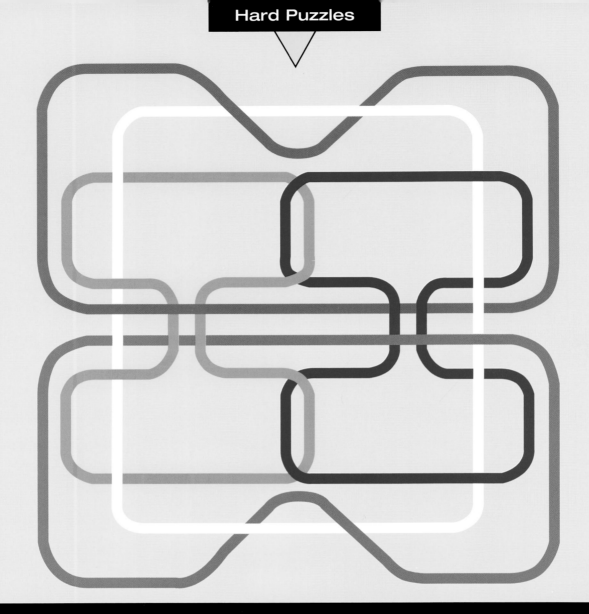

Four of the five rope loops are linked. Which colour loop can be removed without cutting?

46
See answer

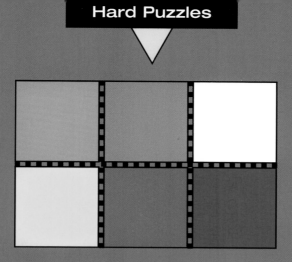

The sheet of paper above is folded along the dotted lines to make a 6 page book. It is bound on one edge and the folds cut so the book can open. Each page is the same colour on both sides. Which one of the books below cannot be made?

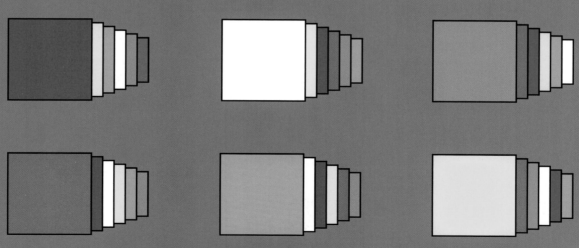

72
See answer

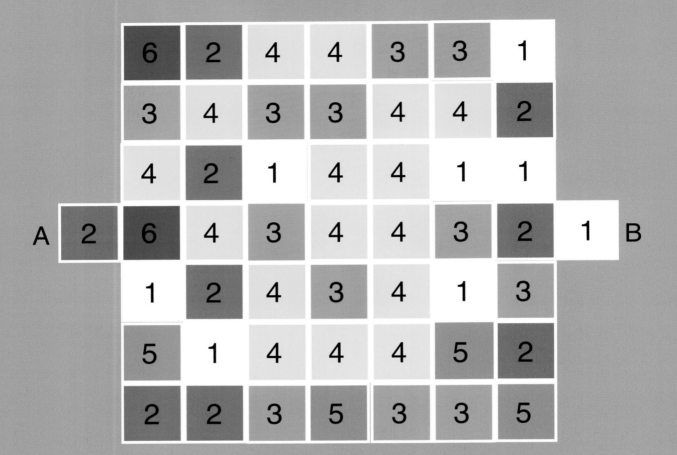

6	2	4	4	3	3	1
3	4	3	3	4	4	2
4	2	1	4	4	1	1
2	6	4	3	4	4	3	2	1
1	2	4	3	4	1	3
5	1	4	4	4	5	2
2	2	3	5	3	3	5

A ... B

Find the shortest route from A to B and then back again.
You can only move the number of squares indicated by the square that you are on.
Moves must be in a straight line, including diagonally.

8
See answer

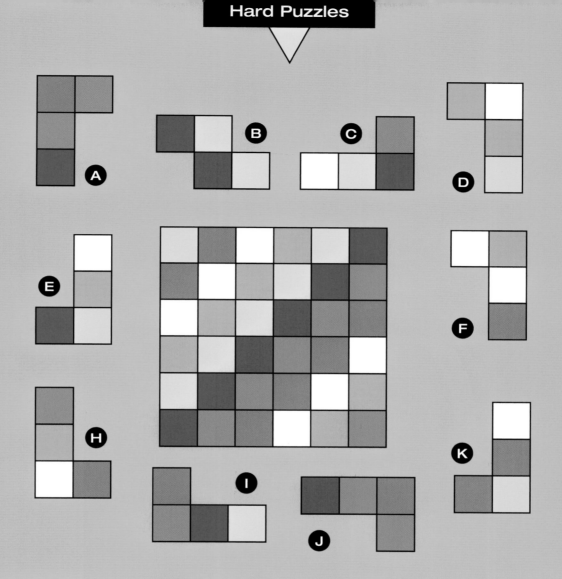

Nine of the ten pieces will fit together to make the square. Which piece is not used?

28
See answer

One ring is rubber. The other five are solid, unbendable metal.
Which is the rubber ring?

81
See answer

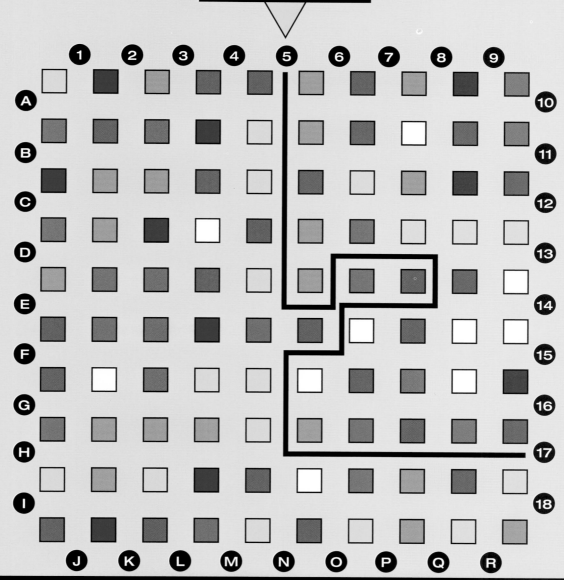

Starting from 5, a path has been drawn through the grid according to certain rules.
If another path were drawn to the same rules starting from H, where would it come out?

102
See answer

These puzzles are of a very different style to the previous puzzles in this book. These eight puzzles are typical examples of the type of puzzles that are solved by the participants of the World Puzzle Championships. The WPCs have been held every year since 1992.

The locations of the WPCs until 1999 were:

1992	New York	USA
1993	Brno	Czech Republik
1994	Cologne	Germany
1995	Poiana Brasov	Romania
1996	Utrecht	The Netherlands
1997	Koprivnica	Chroatia
1998	Istanbul	Turkey
1999	Budapest	Hungary

The 2000 WPC will be held in New York again.

With these eight puzzles you can measure your abilities against the world's best puzzle solvers. If you can solve these puzzles within about 3 hours, you are a first-class puzzle solver, and after some training, you could have a good chance competing against the world's best puzzle minds. As a comparision: the world's best buzzle solvers (like twice world champion Wei-Hwa Huang, Zack Butler, Ron Osher from the USA, Akira Nakai from Japan, Robert Babilon – also twice world champion – from the Czech Republik, Michael Ley from Germany, György István from Hungary, or Pero Galogaza from Croatia) can solve these puzzles in about 90 minutes.

Fill in the square with letters A, B, C, D, and E, so that each letter occurs exactly once in every line and in every column. Three squares in each line and column remain empty. The letters at the sides of the square indicate the letter that can be seen first when looking into the large square from that direction.

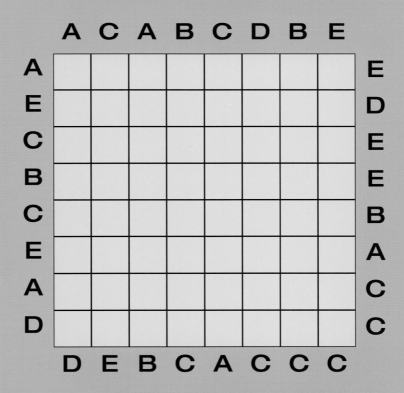

12
See answer

Create six islands in the figure. Each island must consist of six adjoining cells.
The islands do not touch each other, and avoid the dotted cells.

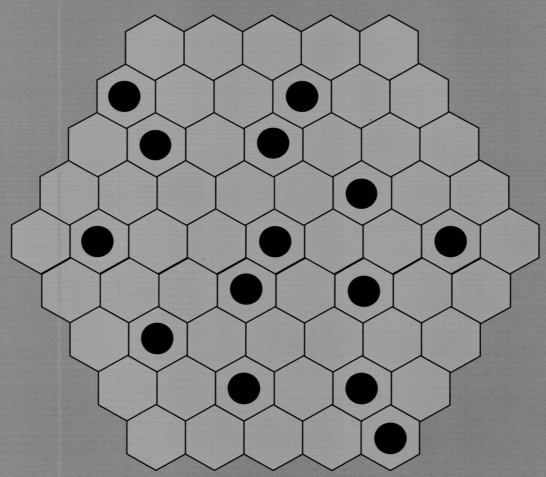

17
See answer

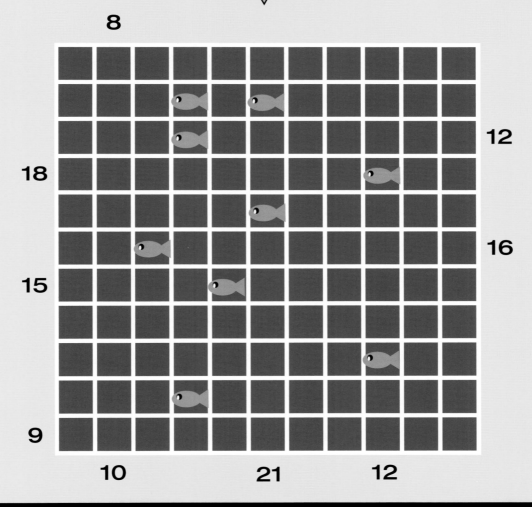

8

12

18

16

15

9

10   21   12

The anglers sit on the shore of the lake represented by the large square.
Each of the anglers has cought one of the fish. The numbers representing the anglers show how
long their line is to their fish. The lines only pass horizontally or vertically through the middle
of the squares, and do not cross each other. Work out which fish belongs to which angler,
and the paths of the lines.

76
See answer

Fill in the square with digits 1 to 9, so that each row, each column, and each of the nine 3x3 squares framed with red lines contains each of the numbers. Some of the numbers are given at the outset.

	3	4		5				
5				1				6
1	8		4		2		7	
7							5	
	1		6		5		3	
	5							2
	2		9		1		8	5
8				2				4
				4		9		

40
See answer

The large square is a radar screen monitoring rainstorms. All the rainstorms are rectangular, and do not touch each other, not even diagonally. The numbers at the edges of the square show the number of squares occupied by rainstorms in that line or column. Find out the exact location of the rainstorms.

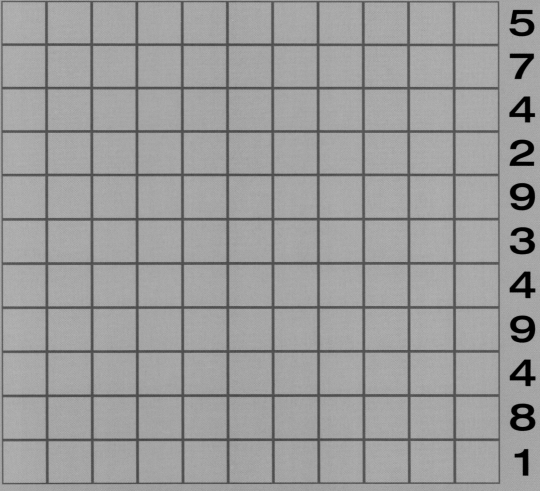

5 7 4 2 9 3 4 9 4 8 1

8 5 6 3 5 9 2 5 6 2 5

7
See answer

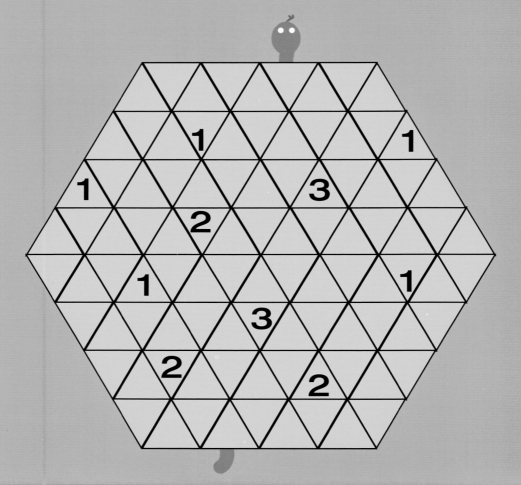

Reconstruct the snake that is hidden in the figure. Only its head and tail are visible.
Each part of the snake passes from the centre point of one side of a triangle to the centre point of
one of the other sides. The snake does not cross itself. In some triangles, the numbers
indicate how many of the adjacent triangles are occupied by the snake. The snake avoids the
triangles with the numbers.

43
See answer

Divide the figure into 20 parts, each consisting of 5 adjacent letters. All the parts must contain each of the letters A, B, C, D, and E.

A	A	E	A	C	D	E	C	B	D
B	E	B	C	D	B	A	D	C	E
E	C	D	A	A	C	A	E	B	B
D	A	E	B	C	B	C	D	E	A
B	C	C	D	A	D	E	C	D	E
D	A	E	E	D	A	E	A	A	D
B	A	B	D	B	C	D	B	C	B
D	C	C	C	C	E	E	B	D	E
A	B	D	A	D	C	E	D	C	C
E	A	B	E	B	A	E	B	A	B

75
See answer

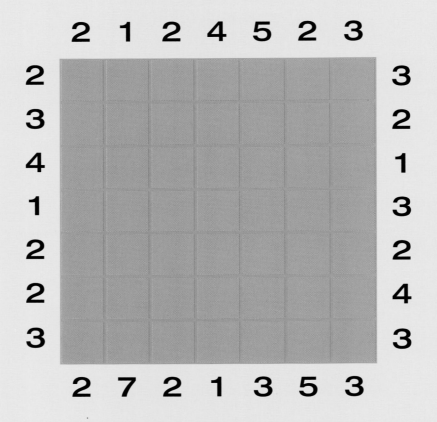

Reconstruct the height of the buildings in this city. Each small square of the city is occupied by a building. The height of the buildings vary between 1 and 7 floors. In every column and in every row the height of each building is different. The numbers at the sides of the city indicate how many buildings are visible from that point when looking to the city in a horizontal or vertical direction. (Note: a higher building hides all the lower ones behind it.)

1

See answer

ANSWERS

Answer 1

	2	1	2	4	5	2	3	
2	6	7	5	2	1	3	4	3
3	1	6	3	4	2	7	5	2
4	2	5	4	6	3	1	7	1
1	7	4	1	3	5	6	2	3
2	4	3	2	1	7	5	6	2
2	3	2	7	5	6	4	1	4
3	5	1	6	7	4	2	3	3
	2	7	2	1	3	5	3	

Answer 2: B.

There are two of each differing feature except: a rim with a single band; a red circle; two bands on the stem; and a blue base. the only goblet to feature all of these is B. It completes the set so that each differing feature occurs exactly twice.

Answer 3: 12 Blue, 24 Red, 14 Green.

A Blue coin equals $1/5$ of an Orange one; 1 Red, $1/40$; and a Green, $1/7$. So if X is the number of Blue coins, Y the Red, and Z the Green, 5 Orange coins equals $X^1/5 + Y^1/40 + Z^1/7$: or when put over a common denominator and multiplying out, $1400 = 56X + 7Y + 40Z$. So 56X and 7Y must be divisible by 10 when added. Trial and error then produces the values of X=12; Y=24; and Z=14 such that X+Y+Z=50.

Answer 4: D.

Let the Red Bar be 1 unit of weight. From the left hand side, a Square equals 2, a Hexagon then equals 5 and the Star 7. On the right, the Circle must now be 3. So 5 weight units are needed, ie a Hexagon.

Answer 5: The Red chest.

If the treasure is in the Blue chest, then all three statements are true. If it is in the Green chest, all three statements are false. If it is the Red chest, then the statement on the Blue chest is false and the other two are true. So the treasure is in the Red chest.

Answer 6: A, D, & E.

Answer 7:

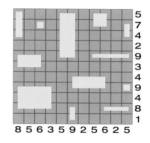

Answer 8:

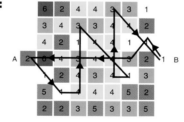

Answer 9: D.

All are rotations of the same figure except for D. (Check the White triangles.)

Answer 11:

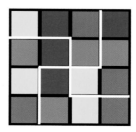

Answer 12:

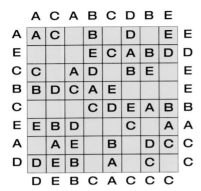

	A	C	A	B	C	D	B	E	
A	A	C		B		D		E	E
E			E	C	A	B	D		D
C	C		A	D		B	E		E
B	B	D	C	A	E				E
C			C	D	E	A	B		B
E	E	B	D			C		A	A
A		A	E		B		D	C	C
D	D	E	B		A		C		C
	D	E	B	C	A	C	C	C	

Answer 13: Orange.
Start from the Green area. Label unknown colours around it as, say, A, B, and C as necessary. You can then work across the map as one or other option will be forced. Eventually, when you reach the other coloured areas, certain colour options will be eliminated. You will then be able to identify the colours of A, B and C and find that the area marked X is Orange.

Answer 14: B & C

Answer 15: Green.
If in doubt, lay some string out according to the diagram (that's what we did). The Green one is the only one that can be removed. Where a loop crosses itself, imagine it turned back so that it doesn't cross. This helps to simplify the picture.

Answer 16: B.

Answer 17:

Answer 18: Blue; Green; White; Yellow; Orange; Red.
Simply work backwards. Red must have been the last placed, Then Orange, and so on back to Blue.

Answer 20: D.

Answer 21: X is Orange, and Y is Red.
There is only one way the map can be coloured such that X and Y are different colours. In this, Y is Red. X must be the same colour as the area that surrounds the Yellow area and is therefore Orange.

Answer 22: The tile immediately to the right of X.
The tile 4th from the left in the top row could be either Yellow or Blue. If it is assumed to be Yellow, the rest of the layout proves impossible, so it is Blue. The rest of the layout can then be deduced apart from X and the tile to the right of it. One is Orange and the other White. So it is only by revealing the one to the right that X can be determined.

Answer 23: 7 Yellow and 1 Blue.
A Yellow weighs $1\frac{4}{11}$ of a Red; a Blue $1\frac{5}{11}$; and a Green, $1\frac{6}{11}$. The number of each must be such that the fractions, when added, are divisible by 11 to give a whole number of Red blocks. There can only be 7 Yellows (giving $9\frac{6}{11}$ Reds); 1 Blue (giving $1\frac{5}{11}$); and no Greens to make a total of 11 Reds.

Answer 24: 9.
In the second diagram, if you put three Red blocks on each scale pan, the left pan is the same as the top diagram. The right scale pans are then equal, that is 12 Green blocks equals 8 Green blocks plus four Red blocks. So a Red block weighs the same as a Green one. Taking three blocks off each side in the top diagram leaves the Yellow ball equal to 9 Green blocks.

Answer 25: Red.
The tile third from left of the fifth row can only be Orange. The first tile in the same row must then be Green. This leads to the identification of other tiles, and so on, to X which must be Red.

Answer 26: 5 Red on the right pan; and 1 Blue on the left.
A Red ball weighs $^{11}/_7$ of a Yellow; a Green, $^{12}/_7$ of a Yellow; and a Blue, $^{13}/_7$ of a Yellow. 6 Yellows equals $^{42}/_7$. If X is the number of Red balls needed, Y the Green, and Z the Blue, the problem is to find X, Y and Z such that $11X+12Y+13Z=42$. Some may be negative (ie, they go on the left pan). The positive values of X,Y and Z must be 6.The only solution is that X=5; Y=0; and Z= -1. So 5 Red are put on the right pan, and 1 Blue on the left.

Answer 27: A.

Answer 28: I.
This is only hard if you do not spot the easy way to solve it. The square contains 6 squares of each colour. However, on the pieces there are 7 Red, 7 Green, 7 Blue, and 7 Yellow. The redundant piece must contain one of each of these colours. The only one is I.

Answer 29: D. (Nobody said it was a horizontal reflection.)

Answer 30: The Orange box.
For the label to be wrong on the Orange box, it must contain two balls of the same colour. By seeing one ball, you will know what it contains. If it is Red, then the Blue box cannot contain two Yellows so must contain one Red and one Yellow and the Green box must contain two Yellows. Similarly, if the ball in the Orange box is Yellow, the Green box contains one Red and one Yellow, and the Blue two Reds.

Answer 31: Red.
The tile fifth from left of the fifth row must be Yellow because if it were Orange there would be no place on the fourth row for an Orange. The fifth from left in the second row is then either White or Orange. White proves to be impossible, so it must be Orange. All the tiles can then be identified.

Answer 32: D.
Only four different patterns can be made by rotating any of the arms through a half circle. D is the fourth.

Answer 33: B.
The colours along the edges of adjacent tiles match. The only one with the right colours to fit the space is B.

Answer 34:

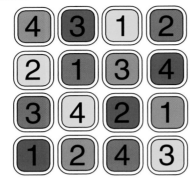

Answer 35:

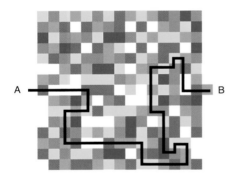

Answer 36: From left to right: White; Orange; Yellow; Green; Red; Blue. Yellow can only be in third position. Then, Red must be in fifth and White and Orange first and second. Green must now be fourth and Blue sixth.

Answer 37: A.
The far right section must equal the right section of the left side. So, using the letters given to the shapes in the question, 2A+D=D+2B+2F. So A=B+F. The bottom lefthand section of the right must equal the bottom right of the left. So 2B+F=B+?. So, the ?=B+F=A. So the missing shape is A, a Blue star.

Answer 38: Red.

Answer 39: D.

Answer 40:

Answer 41: B.
The second figure in both the top pairs is simply the first figure rotated one position anti(counter-)clockwise.

Answer 42: A.

Answer 43:

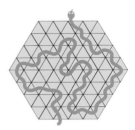

Answer 44:

Answer 45: 7.
From the third weighing, one Blue equals $^3/_4$ of an Orange. In the second weighing, if a Green ball is added to both scale pans, the lefthand one is the same as in the first weighing. So 2 Greens and a Blue equal one Orange. 2 Greens must therefore equal $^1/_4$ of

an Orange, ie, one Green equals $^1/_8$ of an Orange. From the first weighing, a Red ball must equal $^7/_8$ of an Orange, or seven Green balls.

Answer 46: Yellow.
Although the other loops might not seem to pass through one another, they are in fact linked. Only the Yellow loop can actually be removed.

Answer 47: B.
The six circles in the hexagon around each abutting edge must be one of each colour.

Answer 48:

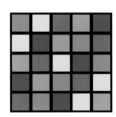

One of first two in the bottom row must be Red. If the second, the other Reds cannot be placed. So the bottom left corner must be Red. All Reds can now be placed. Only Green or Yellow can be in the centre. Whichever it is cannot be in a corner, so Blue and Orange must be in two corners. Blue must be either top right or left. If left, the other Blues cannot be placed. So Blue is top right. All other squares can now be deduced.

Answer 49: B.
In each, Yellow is on top of the Red, which is on Orange, which is on Green, which is on Blue. The exception is B, where Blue is on Green.

Answer 50: H and C.

Answer 51:

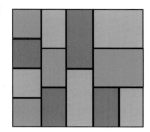

Answer 52:

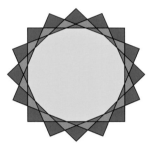

Answer 53: The Yellow key.

Answer 54: F.

Answer 55: A.

Answer 56: D.

Answer 57: C.

Answer 58: B.

Answer 59: E.

Answer 60: C.

Answer 61: B.

Answer 62: Red.

Answer 63: A.

Answer 64: Red.
Wherever you start from, there will be various different ways of colouring the map. Once you reach other areas already coloured, the options will be limited. In the end, there is only one way the map can be coloured, and X is Red.

Answer 65: E.

Answer 66: E.
The are 11 different ways of colouring the triangle with three colours. Ten are shown, the eleventh is E.

Answer 67:

Answer 68:

Answer 69:

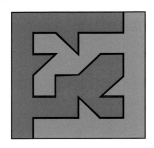

Answer 70:

Answer 71: E.
It is not possible for two colours diagonally adjacent on the sheet to end up as adjacent pages, Red and White in E.

Answer 72: B.
There is only one way of folding the paper so that the first two pages are White followed by Yellow. The other pages will then be, in order, Orange, Green, Red, Blue. So B is not possible. All the others can be folded although a bit of tucking may be required.

Answer 73: C.

Answer 74: The simplest way is if Orange alternates around the middle ring. The rest of the map can then easily be coloured in various ways, one of which is shown here.

Answer 75:

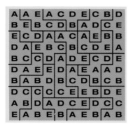

Answer 76: D.

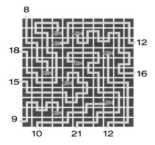

Answer 77: Blue.
All faces of the cube have been shown. There must be two blue faces. If the cube were opened out, it would look like this:

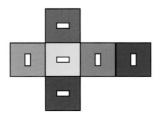

Answer 79: D.
There are two of each colour in each completed row and column. D is the only tile that will finish this pattern.

Answer 80: A and B are diagonal reflections.

Answer 81: Green.
Red is on top of Yellow; Green is on Red; but Yellow is on Green. So one of these three must be flexible. Red is on Orange, and Green is on Red but under Orange. So one of these three must be flexible. Lastly, Blue is on White, and Green is on Blue but under White. So one of these is flexible. The only one common to all groups is Green which must be the rubber ring.

Answer 82: Green.

Answer 83: A.
The entire figure is rotating $\frac{1}{8}$ of a turn clockwise at each step, while the colours of the small circles are switching from circle to circle in the other direction. So A is the missing figure.

Answer 84: D.
Two adjacent colours in the strip cannot appear opposite one another in a four or two colour pattern. So D cannot be made as Yellow and Orange are adjacent in the strip. Any combination of colours is possible in the three colour pattern.

Answer 85:

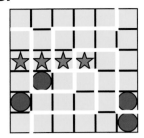

Answer 86: A and C.
For the statement to be true, *all* Red stars must have a Green circle on the reverse. Turning A proves the statement either false if there is a Red circle on the reverse, or possibly true if there is a Green circle. The latter instance can only be confirmed by turning C as it is the only other card that may prove the statement false. If there is a Red star, this shows that the statement is false, if not, it confirms that it is true. Turning D is no help, if there is a Red star on the reverse, it shows the statement may possibly be true. If there is a Green star on the reverse, it proves nothing.

Answer 87: B.

Answer 88: Yellow.

Answer 89: G.
There are four matching pairs: A and H; B and D; C and E; and F and I. G is the odd one.

Answer 90: C.

Answer 91: White
Route tracing problems like this are only possible if all connecting points have an even number of paths from them, or if just two have an odd number. The Yellow, Red, Green and White circles all have an odd number of paths. Since the route must start at Yellow, the new path must connect two of Red, Green or White. As paths may not cross, the only possibility is for a new path to connect White with Red or Green.

Answer 92:
There are two on A; three on B; and one on C.

Answer 93: There would be 21 Red bricks and 13 Blue bricks.
In each new row, there are as many Reds as there were bricks in the previous row, and as many Blues as there were Reds in the previous row. (Actually, each Red brick becomes a Red and a Blue brick on the next row, and each Blue becomes a Red. Done from left to right this generates the 'pattern' of Reds and Blues. This is simply a representation of Fibonacci's 'rabbit' problem that generated the famous Fibonacci series.)

Answer 94: Orange.

Answer 95:

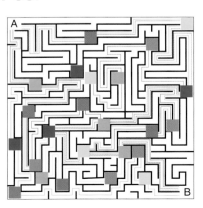

Answer 96:

Answer 97: Avoiding Blue: Orange; Red; Yellow; Green; Yellow; Orange; Red; Orange; Yellow; Red; Orange; B. Avoiding Yellow: Orange; Red; Blue; Green; Orange; Red; Blue; Green; Blue; B. Avoiding Red: Green; Orange; Blue; Yellow; Green; Yellow; Orange; Green; Yellow; Green; Blue; B. Avoiding Orange: Green; Blue; Green; Yellow; Red; Yellow; Green; Yellow; Red; Blue; Yellow; Green; Yellow; Red; Blue; Green; Yellow; Green; Blue; B. Avoiding Green: Orange; Red; Yellow; Blue; Orange; Blue; Orange; Yellow; Red; Blue; Yellow; Orange; Red; Orange; Yellow; Red; Orange; B.

Answer 98: There are several variations of this basic solution.

Answer 99: There are several variations of this basic solution.

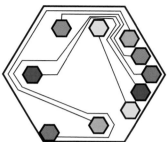

Answer 100: 6.
The rule is to turn right immediately after passing a Yellow, and left after passing a Green. If Green or Yellow is on the corner that was turned, it is ignored in the new direction as it has already had effect.

Answer 101: M.
The rule is that on reaching a junction at which one of the blocks is Red, turn immediately to the side opposite the Red.

Answer 102: B.
The rule is that on reaching each junction: if there are four different colours present in the four surrounding blocks, turn left; if there are only 3 different colours, go straight on; if there are less than three colours present, turn right.

Answer 103: A will descend.
From the first pulley, a Green block equals 1¼ Yellows. So, on the second pulley, 2 Red blocks equal 3¼ Yellows. On the third pulley, side A therefore equals 6¼ Yellows (3¼+3) while B equals 6 Yellows (4x1¼+1). Side A is heavier by a quarter of a Yellow block and so will descend.

Answer 104: Avoiding Red: Blue; Yellow; Green; Blue; Blue; Orange; Blue; Yellow; Blue; Yellow; Blue; Green; Orange; Blue; Yellow; Green; B. Avoiding Blue: Green; Orange; Red; Yellow; Orange; Red; Green; Yellow; Orange; Green; Red; Yellow; Orange; Yellow; Green; Red; Orange; Green; Yellow; Orange; Red; B. Avoiding Orange: Blue; Yellow; Green; Blue; Blue; Yellow; Green; Red; Green; Blue; Yellow left; Blue; Yellow; Green; Red; Green; Red; Blue; Green; Red; Green; Blue; B. Avoiding Green: Yellow; Orange; Red; Orange; Yellow; Blue left; Yellow; Blue; Orange; Blue; Blue; Orange; Red; Blue; Orange; Yellow; Red; Blue; Yellow; Orange; Red; B. Avoiding Yellow; Green; Blue; Orange; Red; Green; Blue; Red; Orange; Red; Green; Blue; Orange; Blue; Blue; Orange; Red; Green; Red; Blue; Green; Red; Green; Blue; B.

Answer 105: Blue and Green.

Answer 106: C.
In the second figure in each pair at the top, each triangle has rotated one position, clockwise then anti-clockwise alternately around the figure from the top triangle. C is the only one of the bottom pairs to conform with this.

Answer 107: Yellow fits in hole C.

Answer 108: Green fits in hole A.

Answer 109: C.

Answer 111: D.
In each row and column, there are three of each shape and three of each colour.

Answer 112: B.
The figures are counting in the binary system (base 2): Blue is 0 or 1, depending on whether it is on or off, Green is 0 or 2; Yellow is 0 or 4; Orange is 0 or 8; and Red is 0 or 16. So twelve would be 8 and 4: Orange and Yellow off and the rest on. Alternatively, you could pick up on the flashing sequences: Blue flashes on and off; Green goes 2 on, 2 off; Yellow, 4 on, 4 off, and so on.